Advance praise fo

127 Unity ? 2

"What is the nature of reality? What are we living for? How can we love? There is no individual, across time and space, whose feet I would rather sit at, exploring such questions, than Jean Vanier. And now, in his ninth decade, he has written this beautiful, searching book in which he takes us by the hand and walks us through these questions as he has lived and embodied and grown into them in the course of an extraordinary life. This book is a gift to us all, as is Jean Vanier himself."

—Krista Tippet, creator and host, *On Being*

"Sentimentality is the great enemy of the good. In this lovely book of hard-won wisdom, Vanier avoids sentimentality by listening to those with mental disabilities. Their fears and courage shape Vanier's soul and this book may even serve to shape ours as well."

—Dr. Stanley Hauerwas, Gilbert T. Rowe Professor Emeritus of Divinity and Law, Duke University

Jean Vanier is a "king of hearts" for our time. Read his beautiful book to refresh your belief in the gentleness of God, in the goodness of all your brothers and sisters, and in the beauty of yourself.

—Timothy P. Shriver, Ph.D. Chairman, Special Olympics International

"*Life's Great Questions* is a rare treasure of 'gold dust,' liberally scattered for life's alert searchers. The reader is enlightened, encouraged, and informed for ever day encounters with love, suffering, evil, goodness, and much, much more."

—Sue Mosteller, C.S.J., friend and colleague

LIFE'S GREAT QUESTIONS

JEAN VANIER

Originally published in the United States of America in 2015
by Franciscan Media, Cincinnati, Ohio

First published in Great Britain in 2016

Society for Promoting Christian Knowledge
36 Causton Street
London SW1P 4ST
www.spck.org.uk

British Library Cataloguing-in-Publication Data
A catalogue record for this book is available from the British Library

ISBN 978–0–281–07595–9
eBook ISBN 978–0–281–07596–6

First printed in Great Britain by Ashford Colour Press
Subsequently digitally printed in Great Britain

eBook by Graphicraft Limited, Hong Kong

Produced on paper from sustainable forests

CONTENTS

This book was written in close collaboration with Janet Whitney-Brown who brought wisdom, insight, and competence to help those who have questions and who are searching to discover the mystery of our world.

By Ronald Rolheiser

The early Church Fathers believed that each of us has two minds and two hearts. Inside each of us, they believed, is a noble, huge mind and heart. But, at the same time, inside us there is also a petty, small mind and heart. For them, this explained the great variations in our feelings and actions, why we can at times be noble, generous, big-hearted, and saintly; just as, at other times, we can be petty, bitter, small-minded, and selfish. Everything depends upon which mind and heart we are operating out of at a given moment. All of Jean Vanier's life, ministry, and work, this book being no exception, are an invitation to us to operate out of our noble mind and big heart. Jean Vanier invites us to what is best in us and to what is best around us.

I first heard Jean Vanier speak when I was a twenty-two-year-old seminarian. For many of my friends, he was a spiritual rock star, but their idolization of him was a negative for me. I went to hear him speak with a certain bias and suspicion: Nobody can be that good! But he was that good!

Admittedly being good is an ambiguous term. What does it mean to be good? Charisma can be as powerful and seductive negatively as it is positively. Someone can be a powerful speaker and motivator without that charisma witnessing at all to that person's human and moral integrity and without that seductiveness inviting those in contact with it to what is higher and more noble. Talent and charisma are ambiguous; they can beckon us toward greatness or seduce us toward selfishness. But Jean Vanier's person, message, and charisma, through more than eighty years, have suffered from no such ambiguity. They have been good in all that is best within that word. The transparency, simplicity, depth, wisdom, and faith contained in his person and his word beckon us in only one direction, namely, toward connecting with our big minds and big hearts, as these already reside inside us and especially in how these exist inside of God. Jean Vanier makes everyone who meets him or his writings want to be a better person. Meeting Jean Vanier makes you want, like the disciples in the Gospels, to leave your boat and net behind and set off on a new, more radical road. And Jean Vanier, himself, models the way.

Perhaps the best criterion by which to judge true, Christian discipleship in our world is to look at who is moving downward. Who fits the description given by St. Paul in the Letter to Philippians when he says of Jesus: "Though he was in the form of God, Jesus did not deem equality with God as something to be grasped at. Rather he emptied himself and took the form of a slave"? Jean Vanier was born into a world of privilege. He was blessed from birth with exceptional parents, a gifted intelligence, a handsome body, enviable educational opportunities, financial security, and a famous name. Those are a lot of gifts for a person to carry and such privilege has as often ruined a life as blessed one. But for Jean Vanier these gifts were never something to be grasped at. Rather, he has constantly emptied himself by immersing himself into the lives of the poor and letting his gifts bless them, even as he has received a rich blessing from them in return: community and happiness. Jean Vanier models what it means to be a true disciple of Jesus.

True discipleship means stepping downward into a second baptism and immersion into the poor. Community and joy are found there. It is to this that he invites us.

Jean Vanier has, through all the years of his long life, stepped through the broken doors of the poor and found there community and joy. This book, *Life's Great Questions*, invites us to search for those doors and it assures us that, once we step through them, our restless search will end. We will be home.

Ronald Rolheiser

San Antonio, Texas

May 28, 2015

That which was from the beginning,
which we have heard,
which we have seen with our eyes,
which we have looked upon and touched with our hands,
concerning the word of life—
...we saw it, and testify to it.
—1 John 1:1

This book is about asking questions. It is about engaging our experience—that which we have "heard," "seen," "looked upon," and "touched"—and daring to ask what it is all about. What are we doing in a world like this? Is my reality the same as that person's reality? Why is there violence? What does it mean to love one another? Who is to blame for the poverty, the environmental destruction, the injustice that I see on television, that I read about in the papers, that I have experienced myself? Where is God in all of this?

We must dare to ask questions! Why is that woman sleeping on the street? What is the difference between "fair trade" and "free trade"? How can I listen to people who don't express themselves with words? What is it that makes me stop when I see the orange and red and purple springing up from a sunset? At what point is it necessary to pick up arms? Where do terrorists come from? What does Jesus mean when he says that those who love their life will lose it (see John 12:25)? What if I don't have any big ambitions about social justice or changing the world?

Questions are like wrestling. We are faced with something unfamiliar, something we don't understand. We can walk away, or we can dare to engage—to challenge ourselves and this unknowing.

There is a wonderful story about wrestling in the first book of the Bible, the book of Genesis. A stranger comes to Jacob in the night, and they wrestle for a long time.

> And Jacob was left alone; and a man wrestled with him until the breaking of the day. When the man saw that he did not prevail against Jacob, he touched the hollow of his thigh; and Jacob's thigh was put out of joint as he wrestled with him. Then he said, "Let me go, for the day is breaking." But Jacob said, "I will not let you go, unless you bless me." And he said to him, "What is your name?" And he said, "Jacob." Then he said, "Your name shall no more be called Jacob, but Israel, for you have striven with God and with men, and have prevailed." Then Jacob asked him, "Tell me, I pray, your name." But he said, "Why is it that you ask my name?" And there he blessed him. (Genesis 32:24–29)

Of course I am not trying to say that we should pounce upon every stranger that we come across. What I am saying is that when we have an experience that is a little shocking, a little extraordinary, we should not put it out of our minds. We should engage it until we have come to some revelation. The first revelation in this story is that of Jacob himself. "Your name shall no more be called Jacob, but Israel." In wrestling, in asking questions and pushing the boundaries of what we know and what is familiar, we will come to know ourselves better as well.

The second revelation is that of the stranger. "And he said to him, 'What is your name?' And he said, 'Jacob.' Then he said, 'Your name shall no more be called Jacob, but Israel, for you have striven with God and with men, and have prevailed.'" Jacob realizes that it is God. But God's full identity is not bared. Mystery endures. And although we may not have found a solution, we will always receive something—a greater awareness, a broader understanding of reality, a grace to continue on our way. "And there he blessed him."

This is not a book about answers. One question leads to another and another, taking us on a journey. It is not about defining but discovering, a pilgrimage of thoughts and ideas. It is about you and I traveling on a road together, exploring notions of love, greed, hatred, freedom, God, and humanity. It is a book about engaging and wrestling with reality, searching for the truth. Mystery is always present, inviting us forward.

At the beginning of the Gospel of John, two young men follow Jesus. Perhaps they are hoping for some answers. Perhaps they are a little taken aback when he turns to them and says, "What do you want?" They respond with a question of their own: "Where do you live?" (John 1:38, NJB)? Jesus replies with an invitation, an invitation to live something new, to leave what is normal, what is familiar, and take a path toward something new and unexpected, a journey of human growth.

I hope that this will be our experience also as we journey from one question to the next, exploring our life experiences, exploring the Gospels, revealing something about who we are, revealing something about the life that we live.

"He replied, 'Come and see'; so they went..." (John 1:39, NJB).

CHAPTER ONE

Where Do Ideas Come From?

In 1964 I visited an institution in a little village in France. It was a place for people that society called "imbeciles, idiots, crazy." It was supposed to hold forty people—which was already quite a lot. But in response to the overwhelming need, there were eighty people living there. Their beds were crammed one against the other; their meals were chaotic and loud. This was not a life—it was a minimal existence; it was all that was allotted for people with minimal value in a world of competence and competition, egocentrism and efficiency, price tags and predictability. Was this institution "helping"? One could say that it was helping the parents who didn't know what else to do with their children. One might even venture that it was helping the state that needed to get these people off the street. But this institution was not helping men and women with intellectual disabilities.

How could such a place exist? Was it the fault of parents who were not able to accept or care for their child? Was it the fault of the government who did not find the money to offer the right resources and support? Who was responsible for helping them?

The ninth chapter of the Gospel of John opens with a similar question. "Who sinned, this man or his parents, that he should have been born blind?" ask Jesus's disciples as they walk past a man begging in the street. Their question assumes that a disability is directly related to sin. Our questions above assume that we must be in a helping relationship with a person with a disability. In many ways we live in a very narrow world, one of black and white, rich and poor, right and wrong, ability and disability.

Ideas come when we are seeking freedom. We cannot live in a closed reality. We must find new ways of meeting one another so as to become free of the restrictive identities and barriers that keep us apart.

Jesus replies, "Neither he nor his parents sinned…he was born blind so that the works of God might be revealed in him" (John 9:2–3, NJB). It is an astonishing answer, one that turns the world upside down. Not only is his blindness independent of fault or guilt, it is a gift! It is an instrument "so that the works of God might be revealed in him."

I am going to say something strange. Here, among these men who had nothing to do during the day, who were crying out, I felt a mysterious attraction. I have visited prisons and slums, psychiatric hospitals and refugee camps, leper colonies, and many other institutions for people with disabilities. They are horrible places, and part of me wants to turn away. But at the same time, I am also drawn to these places. It is a paradox. The image of Jesus upon the cross is also a paradox. It is life in death, serenity in suffering, dignity in humiliation, power in abandonment. This too is compelling. Why is that? It is as if in the heart of the anguish, there is a mysterious presence. Paradox reveals truth that can hardly be spoken; it is something invisible, and yet it is there.

Ideas come from a world turned upside down. We have heard wisdom from someone we were told was foolish. We have experienced generosity from someone who seems to have nothing, and we have experienced misery in someone who seems to have it all. We have suddenly understood that there is a gift in disability. Ideas help us to take in the contradiction that is reality.

Let's imagine for a moment what it is to be like that man and sitting on a beach. Close your eyes. Sitting on the ground, you can feel that there is sand beneath you. It is almost like water except that it catches under your fingernails and seems to harden under your seat. There is a smell, pungent but fresh, carried on a breeze. You breathe in, as if drinking this wind. It is cold. Licking your lips, you discover that they are salty. Another breath. You become conscious that your breaths are controlled by a rhythm that surrounds you. First a long draw, like dragging feet across graveled walkways. You are inhaling. And then a terrible crash, the sound of a dish slipping out of your hands over and over and over again. Over and over you brace yourself for fear of something you cannot understand.

Open your eyes.

The brilliance is overwhelming, the vastness of it all. Who knew that the world was so big! Suddenly everything comes together, the sand that stretches out toward the water, dragged in a long inhale out toward that great expanse of blue. The sand is forgotten as the water is gathered up, towering in cobalt, turquoise, and pearl. The wind catches drops from the top and suddenly you know where that taste comes from. And then with unimaginable grace and power, the wave breaks, racing along the sand in foamy current. You jump up laughing as the water only just catches the tips of your toes. You spread your arms wide taking it all in, inhale and exhale fading into the vastness overhead… how small you are and how free!

> [Jesus] spat on the ground, made a paste with the spittle, put
> this over the eyes of the blind man, and said to him, "Go and

wash in the Pool of Siloam" (the name means 'one who has been sent'). So he went off and washed and came back able to see. (John 9:6–7, NJB)

Idea comes from the Greek—*idein*, meaning, "to see," a moment of nonverbalized clarity. We can navigate in this upside-down world. Something seems to have become clear.

When the blind man comes back, people are shocked and amazed. They cannot believe it!

"Isn't this the man who used to sit and beg?" Some said, "Yes, it is the same one." Others said, "No, but he looks just like him." The man himself said, "Yes, I am the one." So they said to him, "Then how is it that your eyes were opened?" He answered, "The man called Jesus made a paste, daubed my eyes with it and said to me, 'Go off and wash at Siloam'; so I went, and when I washed I gained my sight." They asked, "Where is he?" He answered, "I don't know." (John 9:8–12, NJB)

Ideas come from searching, from asking questions. We must not walk away from our paradoxical experiences, but accept them and seek to situate them in a more truthful understanding of the world. How? Who? Where? Why?

When I was young, I did a lot of searching. As I will describe later, I left the military where I had become quite respected as a naval officer on board of Canada's only aircraft carrier at the time. But something was growing within me, a deep attraction toward prayer, toward attending Mass, toward being with the poor, toward a vision of community that I had seen in a movie when I was younger. It was something that I could not quite articulate, but I knew that it was real. I handed in my resignation.

When the blind man from the Gospel story returns to the temple, the people want to know what has happened. They want this miracle to be explained in such a way that they can understand. "They brought to the Pharisees the man who had been blind." Pharisees are the holders of the law, the ones who know inside and out all the structures by which to understand every aspect of living. And so the discussion enters into the legal framework of that time. "Some of the Pharisees said, 'That man cannot be from God: he does not keep the Sabbath.' Others said, 'How can a sinner produce signs like this?' And there was division among them" (John 9:13, 16, NJB).

Ideas come from a necessity to overcome divisions, to live something new. People have said that those with disabilities are no good. And yet experience tells us that they are unique and important to the world. How to overcome the division between experience and what is thought to be normal? Religious faith can separate us also. But we can overcome these divisions by sharing our human experiences of life, suffering, and death.

After resigning from the navy, I met someone who guided me in my searching, someone very wise whose life and philosophy spoke to me. By his recommendation I completed a doctorate in philosophy on the topic of happiness with reference to the work of Aristotle. I was given a teaching position at the University of Toronto. Although living in a prestigious academic setting, I continued to be drawn to people like Tony Walsh and Dorothy Day.

In the 1930s, Dorothy Day, a journalist in New York City, began a newspaper to promote Catholic social teachings—pacifism, social justice, and community. In 1933 she and her friend, Peter Maurin, began a little autonomous community with a mission of hospitality and social justice in light of the fundamental dignity of every human person. Day's vision not only put her on the periphery of mainstream society, it also put her at odds with the Catholic Church. For example, in 1951, because of her criticism of the Church's lack of sympathy for striking cemetery workers, she was told to remove the word "Catholic" from the name of the publication. However, the hierarchy of the Church did not intimidate Day, and *Catholic Worker* continued unchanged. Today there are many Catholic Worker communities around the United States.

Tony Walsh was instrumental in founding a similar house in Montreal, Canada. The Benedict Labre House also has a mission of service to the poor and social justice. Like the Catholic Worker, the local Catholic community regarded Benedict Labre House with some suspicion. The project did not have the recognition of the archdiocese and seemed to bear some resemblance to a communist experiment. Walsh chose to live a life of poverty so as to truly be with the people being served. I knew Walsh personally and was greatly inspired. Day, Walsh, and many others who do similar work are courageous. They have dared to leave their familiar milieus and possibilities of conventional success, trusting in something that they know to be true and just.

Each of us has an opportunity in little ways to live justice and peace. But it takes daring; it is a risk. The man born blind is less intimidated.

> "What have you to say about him yourself, now that he has opened your eyes?" The man answered, "He is a prophet." However, the [authorities] would not believe that the man had been blind without first sending for the parents of the man who had gained his sight and asking them, "Is this man really

the son of yours who you say was born blind? If so, how is it that he is now able to see?" His parents answered, "We know he is our son and we know he was born blind, but how he can see, we don't know, nor who opened his eyes. Ask him. He is old enough: let him speak for himself." His parents spoke like this out of fear of the [authorities], who had already agreed to ban from the synagogue anyone who should acknowledge Jesus as the Christ. This was why his parents said, "He is old enough; ask him." (John 9:17–23, NJB)

Sometimes, like these parents, we can be afraid to see that people who are poor, who are rejected by society, who have disabilities all have something fundamental to teach us about what it is to be human. We can be enclosed within walls of fear. We have a fear of difference or strangeness. And even more fundamentally, we have a fear of discovering that we are not so different after all.

So the [authorities] sent for the man again and said to him, "Give glory to God! We are satisfied that this man is a sinner." The man answered, "Whether he is a sinner I don't know; all I know is that I was blind and now I can see." (John 9:24–25, NJB)

What does it take to witness uncompromisingly to the truth? What does it take to say, "I was blind and now I can see"?

Ideas come when we dare to live courageously, when we are willing to accept risk in pursuit of what is true, when we are willing to express our experiences, to witness to them and help others to do the same. Newness is always a risk. And yet, we contextualize the paradox of our experiences by the realization of something new. Newness is the way of truth. It is the way of peace.

When my friend became chaplain to an institution of about thirty men in a little village in France, I knew that I would go there to be with him. What a crazy idea! Were my parents a little bit concerned? Probably. Was the university a little bit surprised? I would imagine so. But for me it was obvious. I invited Raphael and Philippe, two men from the institution, to come and live with me in a run-down little house in this little village. And so L'Arche began!

> They said to him, "What did he do to you? How did he open your eyes?" He replied, "I have told you once and you wouldn't listen. Why do you want to hear it all again? Do you want to become his disciples yourselves?" At this they hurled abuse at him, "It is you who are his disciple…we don't know where he comes from." The man replied, "That is just what is so amazing!" (John 9:26–30, NJB)

Sometimes it is difficult to explain what L'Arche is. In more formal language, we are people with and without intellectual disabilities living mutually transforming relationships in communities that become signs of peace in the world. We discover that, although some of us may have come to assist or help the core members, we too are changed. We become more patient, more kind, more accepting, more forgiving, more joyful. In short, we learn to love. This is so important to recognize. But we mustn't stop there! We must also express, as the blind man dares to do, what is happening to us.

> "You don't know where he comes from and he has opened my eyes! We know that God doesn't listen to sinners, but God does listen to people who are devout and do his will. Ever since the world began it is unheard of for anyone to open the

eyes of someone born blind; if this man were not from God, he wouldn't have been able to do anything." They retorted, "Are you trying to teach us, and you a sinner through and through ever since you were born!" And they ejected him. Jesus heard they had ejected him, and when he found him he said to him, "Do you believe in the Son of man?" "Sir," the man replied, "tell me who he is so that I may believe in him." Jesus said, "You have seen him; he is speaking to you." The man said, "Lord, I believe," and worshipped him. (John 9:30–38, NJB)

Ideas come with humility. It is when we are open to reality, when we have let go of pretense and the desire to control or explain, that we can welcome our experience and the truth that is revealed there. "The Word of life—this is our theme" (1 John 1:1, NJB).

Let us see what we have discovered. Ideas are about freedom. They are about wrestling, about the world turning upside down, about seeing, about searching, about overcoming divisions, about courage, and about humility. They come from our experiences.

Perhaps most importantly, ideas come from reality—from having our awareness firmly in the world around us. We are living in a tension of our heart and our head, of our head and our experience, and of our heart and experience. We see one thing and yet feel something different than what we see. We anticipate one thing and then experience it completely otherwise. We rationalize, and yet it still feels wrong.

Ideas are about harmonizing our hearts, heads, and experience. Ideas are about finding unity so that we can live in reality. This brings us to our next question. What is reality?

CHAPTER TWO

What Is Reality?

Let us begin by looking at the world around us. John in his first letter justifies the authenticity of his witness of the "Word made flesh" because it is that "which we have heard, which we have seen with our own eyes, which we have watched and touched with our own hands" (1 John 1:1, NJB). This is reality. We hear it, see it, watch and touch it, smell it, and feel it.

Let me begin by telling you about what I have seen myself. I had to go to Chile for a meeting where we were going to discuss the incredible gifts of people with disabilities. I arrived at the airport and I was met by Denis, a wonderful man. He was to drive me to Santiago, the capital. On the way, he slowed down. He said, "Here, if you look to the left, you have all the slum areas of the city; and on the right, you have all the rich houses protected by the military and the police." And then he added, "Nobody crosses that road."

Let us begin there, with this terrible division between the rich and the poor.

Jesus speaks in the sixteenth chapter of the Gospel of Luke about a man called Lazarus who was sitting on the ground, covered in sores (see Luke 17:19–31). Lazarus probably had leprosy. Just across the way, there was a man who was having big feasts in his house. The food would fall from his table, and the dogs would eat it. Did this man, who had so much food that it was spilling onto the floor, simply not see Lazarus who had nothing?

Let us look at the world around us and see that there are over one billion people living in slums in the world. Have you ever seen a slum? It can be very surprising the first time. It is hard to believe that families live in these broken-down lodgings. The houses tend not to have a second story since building materials are quite simple. And so slum areas stretch out low over large areas in a labyrinth of human activity.

Once I was driven past a slum area in Brazil. "The government has tried to relocate these people," I was told, "but they don't want to go. Why would they want to leave their community and live separated from one another in little apartments? But the government wants them to move away from the edge of the city where the slum is so visible. If they are in apartments, no one will see them anymore."

So often the division between rich and poor is reinforced with barriers that keep us comfortably ignorant of one another. We create walls so that we cannot see across the road, so that we are not even aware of Lazarus with his hand outstretched, so that we are protected from the reality of our dividedness and the responsibility that we might have in front of those who are in dire need.

The fullness of reality can be difficult to face. Sometimes we protect ourselves with compulsions, numbing our capacity to see, hear, watch, touch, smell, and even feel. Some people work incessantly so that they are never quite in reality. Some people spend mindless hours on the Internet; others spend hours in front of the television or playing games. Some people shop compulsively. Some people are always alone and never attend social events; other people cannot stand to miss a single social event and are always planning the next one.

One man that I know developed a habit of getting up as soon as he was finished with his meal to blow his nose. It happened once or twice while he had a cold, and so we thought nothing of it. But then we noticed that he got up immediately after every meal. It was a way of coping with the reality that he had eaten more quickly than everyone and now had to wait. The thought of the Kleenex box filled his mind.

Compulsions often begin as a natural behavior, but later they may take over and control us. Compulsions create a sort of virtual world that protects us—even unintentionally—from the fullness of reality. We may look at a Facebook profile twenty times a day and not once look at the news headlines. We might send a friend request to someone we hardly know but never make eye contact with someone on the bus. We may donate hundreds of dollars to a charitable organization but never offer even a smile to a person begging on the street. We may serve food at a soup kitchen for years but never sit down to share the meal. Compulsions may fill a void without solving the reason for our emptiness, the way that eating a bag of chips might fill our bellies but not diminish our hunger.

Walls that restrict our reality can also take the form of protective narratives—stories that we tell ourselves to justify our dividedness. "I could take more time to read the headlines, but I can't do anything about it anyway so there's no point." "If I make eye contact, that person might think I am creepy." "The person begging just wants a couple of dollars to buy a beer." "Aren't I a wonderful person for serving up soup at a soup kitchen?" "I could take more time to volunteer, but I need to focus on my studies so that I can effect *real* change in the world."

It is astonishing how detached we can become from reality. Communism, for example, is, in and of itself, a beautiful vision of people living together, sharing their life and wealth. But the reality is a concentration of power, increasing poverty and oppression, and the manipulation of an ideal to serve the ambitions of a few.

Other narratives have been even more destructive. In Canada, the government had a vision of First Nations people being integrated into "normal" society. Nicholas Flood Davin, commissioned by Prime Minister Sir John A. MacDonald, wrote in 1879 that "if anything is to be done with the Indian, we must catch him very young. The children must be kept constantly within the circle of civilized conditions."[1] From the 1880s until the late twentieth century, schools were publicly funded and run by Roman Catholic, Anglican, Presbyterian, and United Churches. In 1920, the Indian Act prohibited a First Nations child from attending any educational institution other than these residential schools. To this end, they were separated from their families, stripped of their language and culture, and in some cases exposed to situations of physical and sexual abuse. Contrary to the aim of any good school, most students reached only a grade five level by the time they were eighteen. Over 150,000 First Nation, Metis, and Inuit children passed through these schools. In 2007, residential school "survivors," as they are called, took the government and associated churches to court. The Indian Residential Schools Settlement Agreement is the largest class-action settlement in Canadian history. In 2008 the prime minister issued a formal apology to these survivors.[2] A large sum of money was mandated for reparations to students who directly suffered from the effects of residential schools. Moreover, the agreement launched a Truth and Reconciliation Commission (TRC), with the mission of hearing the truth of what happened and moving toward healing.

Healing our reality means breaking out of the narratives that protect and limit us. The TRC is about exposing the incredible injustice that lies behind what was and still is perceived as normal. Today there are no more residential schools. But the narrative of inferiority and the consequent segregation persists. We cannot live in reality until we are free of embedded judgments and racism so that we can accept our neighbors as they are, not seeking to change them or to become the same, but celebrating together our differences and our humanity.

In Jesus's time, normality was prescribed by the Law, which was a very powerful and limiting structure that tightly controlled people's sense of the world. Throughout the Gospels, Jesus runs into conflict with the authorities—the Pharisees and the Sadducees—because he challenges the laws that have been put in place to direct people's faith practice and living. In the second chapter of the Gospel of John, he goes into the Temple and sees a marketplace. Specific rules about animals to be sacrificed and an economy had developed around the marketplace. There was even a financial system with moneychangers who would exchange other currencies for Temple money. You can imagine the possibilities for making a profit off the top, all within the narrative of religious devotion. Jesus goes in and upends tables; he drives out the animals and scatters coins all over the ground. "Stop using my Father's house as a market," he says (John 2:16, NJB). His words shake the structures and norms, revealing the reality of injustice and hypocrisy being lived out.

This question of what is reality is essential. We must be careful not to be enclosed within a narrow perception of the world. We must not be led to believe that reality is what is on my side of the road, that it is confined to these protective walls, to the expectations of our families and friends, to what is normal in our society or our religion. We must dare to break free of our limited sense of the world. Of course it is not easy, but so often we do not even make the effort.

Let me try to explain this more concretely. For fifty years I have lived in community with people with intellectual disabilities. When L'Arche began in 1964, people with disabilities tended to be placed in institutions or hospices, pushed away by society. Institutions seemed to be doing a service to parents by taking the burden of their disabled child off their hands. Today there have been many advances, but people with disabilities are still pushed to the margins. They, in their abnormality, present a startling challenge to mainstream society. They are so different from us. What they touch, see, smell, hear, and feel can seem to have little in common with able-bodied experiences. Often we can be afraid to be with them. We cannot understand their behavior, their bodies seems strange, their words incomprehensible. "What does their reality have to do with mine?" we might ask.

Assistants that come to our community will find that they are standing on the edge of the road between normality and a sort of craziness. It is much like the road in Santiago. Looking at the other side can be very startling. As we stand on our side of the road, we might wonder what good it does to take a step across. Perhaps we ought to take care of them because they are human beings, we think, but we are not sure that they are worth anything. Whose fault is it that they are on the wrong side of the road?

In time, living together, the assistant will find that it *is* possible, even enjoyable, to sit together, to share a meal, a joke, or even a difficult moment. Little by little, as we dare to be with the person who is very different from us, we become accustomed to one another's presence and we learn to listen deeply. And there is the destabilizing discovery that these people—people whom we thought to be no good, deficient, and useless—are important. They have something to teach us about presence, about taking time with one another, about growing together, about accepting vulnerability and weakness so that we can be together in truth. We discover that reality is not simply the so-called normality that we knew growing up, nor is it that craziness that startles us initially. The reality is that these worlds are divided, but they need not be. Reality is that contradiction, and there is truth.

And so reality is about truth. It is about the *wholeness* of what is seen, heard, touched, smelled, and felt, as John says. It is about taking in everything around us and being open to another's point of view, another's experience. Reality is the rich *and* the poor, the disability *and* the ability, the slums *and* the suburbs, the joy *and* the suffering, the grief *and* the celebration.

If we are to know reality, we must be willing to cross the road, to break down the walls, to push over the barriers that exist between us and, as we will discover, that also exist within us.

CHAPTER THREE

Why Is There So Much Suffering?

When we are young, we may not be aware of suffering in the world. We may experience disappointments, difficulties at school or at home, even sad occasions. We might have seen images on television about poverty in other parts of the world. We have probably walked by people who are homeless. But we may not be able to integrate these brushings with hardship until we ourselves have lived something similar. As we grow a little older, we have probably lived enough to know what suffering is. Perhaps the loss of a grandparent gives us a taste of the experience of others who have lost family members. Perhaps a friend's parents are no longer together and we touch the complex distress of a broken family. Perhaps we have been in a relationship and experienced what it is to have one's heart broken. When we have suffered, we can become aware of and be touched by the immense suffering around us. We will certainly be led to the question "Why is there so much suffering?"

There are some causes of suffering that we have little control over. People fall sick, accidents happen, natural disasters wreak havoc. Why is it that one person has cancer and another does not? Why is it that some people live on a fault line or in a zone that is especially at risk from tsunamis? Why is there such a thing as an Ebola virus? There is no answer to these questions. We are part of nature, subject to its laws and movement. Although it is always good to ask why, sometimes we must accept that we cannot fully understand. What is important is how we live with these events. Someone who seemed perfectly balanced suddenly has a schizophrenic episode. It is scary! We wonder: Why did it happen? Is it someone's fault?

In many cases, this question of why there is so much suffering is difficult to address. We do better asking, "How can I live in such a way that this suffering becomes a source of life? How can I love this person in their fragility, in their time of need? How can I help them to see that they are beloved and precious? How can life spring from disaster?" Perhaps a community is drawn together in the wake of a hurricane. Sickness and death are often times of incredible pain, but they can also be amazing passages: sacred times when we are reminded of the wonder of life and the importance of presence.

Some kinds of suffering are within our control. If we are willing to grow, we can do a lot to alleviate suffering in ourselves and in the world around us. For example, let's return to the problem of barriers. Why is there is so much suffering? It has something to do with the dividedness of our reality, the walls we hide behind, and the barriers that separate us. When there are barriers, we are unable to see the people on the other side of the street. Lazarus was hungry. The rich man had excessive amounts of food. But when people remain locked away from each other, there is suffering.

The reality is that there are many divisions. The rich are separated from the poor, the "normal" from the "abnormal," the young from the old, the successful from the unsuccessful. We might also see a growing separation between our societies and the earth upon which we depend. Our closest relationship with the earth is of course our connection with food. And yet in our modern world we may associate food with a supermarket rather than with sun and rain, with harvests and changing seasons. Meat consumption is increasing, and yet the steak in the freezer rarely reminds us of a four-legged creature with enormous eyes and a curious tongue.

Divisions and walls mean that we can cause pain or suffering without ever being aware that we are doing so. Very few of us have seen the factories where our clothing is made. Are we aware of the women in Bangladesh who work long hours in appalling working conditions with minimal safety standards so that we can buy an inexpensive shirt? Very few of us understand the delicate balance that determines the hospitality of our climate and the frequency of dangerous storms, droughts, and extreme temperatures. Few of us will face rising sea levels. How can we become conscious of the environmental impact of getting in a car, of taking an airplane, of turning up the thermostat? Even in schools, there is division. In much of Germany, students are divided into different types of school depending upon their academic performance. This happens at the end of grade four! I remember one young mother asking another one in Canada, where students are not sorted in this way, "But how can your child learn, with those *other* kids in the classroom?"

Many people have not met people with intellectual disabilities. So how can they be aware of the anguish that these men and women experience when they are put into institutions, when they are marginalized? How can they know their feeling of deep loneliness and abandonment? How can they understand the suffering imposed by a society whose values of academic merit and financial success, and whose norms seem to have little correspondence with the world of people with disabilities?

This terrible division may allow us to assume that to have a disability is in itself such a suffering that it is better to kill a child with a disability before he or she is born.

I would like to tell you another story. Anthony, a man that I used to live with in L'Arche, would often fall over. He would trip over nothing at all, hitting the ground multiple times a day. The assistants told me, "It is normal. He falls over all the time. He must learn to stay on his feet. There is no sense in helping him back up again." It was not nice to see him on the ground. It required some "wall making" to ignore his cry for help.

Perhaps the rich man looked out at Lazarus and said, "That poor man. Why can't he just pluck up the courage to go out and look for a job? Why can't he stop drinking and start to make something of his life instead? Why is he so lazy?" It required some "wall-making" to be able to refuse to meet and speak to Lazarus, to eat at his well-laden table. I imagine the rich man tried to avoid seeing Lazarus so as to avoid the suffering he would feel.

No one rejoices when they see poverty or weakness. I suffered watching Anthony fall again and again. Some felt that Anthony was capable of getting up on his own, but I felt that Anthony's falling was a cry for help: "Does anyone want to help me?" So one day, I put out my hand and helped Anthony up. After that, his compulsive falling ended.

Divisions make it easy to impose suffering on others without ever facing the consequences. And when we *do* face the consequences, they can be so difficult, so seemingly unreal, that we cannot accept them. When suffering is evoked in us, we try to protect ourselves by reinforcing division. This is a vicious cycle. The more the rich man refuses to accept his participation in Lazarus's poverty by exercising his greed, the hungrier Lazarus becomes. The hungrier Lazarus becomes, the more disturbed and defensive the rich man becomes, and so on and so forth. To go across and invite Lazarus to his table is a risk. It is also painful because the rich man will be faced with the consequences of his greed. But it is the way to end this cycle of suffering.

This might lead us to another question. Are pain and suffering the same? Pain seems more acute. We can step on a nail, there is pain, and we may suffer from that pain. We may lose a family member and suffer that loss. We fail an exam and suffer humiliation. Suffering implies enduring or undergoing hardship. There are many sources of suffering that we cannot understand.

Would we say that a woman suffers childbirth? It is certainly very painful. But can we also say that her suffering is alleviated by the miracle of giving life? I don't know.

Perhaps we can say that our suffering is more or less dependent on our capacity to contextualize it. When we can understand or rationalize a loss, our well-being is less affected. Pain, loss, humiliation—these are all part of reality, part of the human experience. But how much we *suffer* pain may depend upon our ability to see the whole picture: our ability to accept, for example, that although there is pain now, soon there will be a new child.

We might make the distinction between pain and suffering by seeing that pain is like the aching legs and scorching heat we experience on a long walk in the desert. But the suffering is far greater if we are lost.

Contextualizing means finding where we are on the map. It means discovering a movement of life and becoming aware of certain laws of nature. I think that we try to do this. When we are faced with disasters, pain, difficulties, and challenges, we tell stories so that we can make sense of things. Sometimes we learn how to live more harmoniously with the people around us, with the world around us. We create structures such as traditions, cultural norms, protocols, and laws so as to position ourselves. We do manage to reduce suffering because we know how to avoid some sources of it. And we alleviate it because we know what to expect when we *do* experience pain.

Let us never forget that structures are a *simplification* of reality. Although useful in orienting us, structures are defined: there are boundaries. And if there is a boundary, we can be within the boundary or outside of the boundary, which means that there is division. Reality can never be confined to that which we understand. We must be wary of clichés and simplifications, of explanations and attempts to verbalize that which is beyond words. These are crutches: helpful to walk a few steps, but potentially restrictive and divisive. In the process of intellectualizing reality, we reduce it.

I will tell you another story. I watched the children of a friend of mine playing together in the family living room. At one point, as often happens, the older one (about six years old) decided that he had had enough. He lay on the couch to read a comic book. The younger one clearly thought this was a poor idea. He crept up on this brother and tickled his toes. You can imagine the agitation, which grew into a fury as the little brother persisted, coming back a dozen times. "Go away!" the older brother yelled in vain. Finally the older brother got down onto the carpet. Have you ever drawn pictures in a carpet? Often the threads are all pushed in one direction and if you drag your finger against the grain, you can succeed in making a visible line. This is what the older brother did. "Look," he said, "that is your side and this is mine. If you come across the line, I will be really, really mad."

It seemed like a good idea, a boundary. It was a boundary, kind of like the one for Anthony: so long as he keeps falling, there is nothing to do for him. It was a boundary, kind of like the one for Lazarus: so long as he does not pick himself up off the sidewalk, I cannot invite him into my home.

In the living room, a line in the carpet made conflict all the more simple. Now the little brother had to put only one toe across and his brother would leap from the sofa steaming. Forget about peacefully reading his comic book, there was a boundary to defend! I went away for a little while, and when I came back, I saw the two of them curled up together on the sofa reading together. The line was nowhere to be seen.

We have seen by now how barriers and divisions cause suffering. And we have seen how the breaking down of barriers and the overcoming of division works to alleviate suffering in ourselves and in others. How can we understand this? Perhaps it is as simple as recognizing that, as much as he might try to deny it, the rich man is in relationship with Lazarus. However far away that woman in Bangladesh who sowed my shirt seems, I am in relationship with her. However easily I can forget the climate change studies or the witness of people whose living situations are threatened by rising tides, we live on the same earth. However different from me that person with a disability, however strange her reasoning, her way of communicating, however peculiar her body, we are part of one human family.

In the United States (and elsewhere), black people have been treated as insignificant. They have been assumed to be inferior. Even after it was accepted that they should not be enslaved, racism continued cruelly. Segregation policies separated white people from colored in the educational system, in the military, in marriage, in sports, in public transportation, in washroom facilities, even in restaurants and concert halls. Black people suffered not only from the feeling of being different and rejected, but also from appalling physical violence. They were forced to work and live in dangerous and humiliating situations. It is astonishing that a country founded upon the "life, liberty, and the pursuit of happiness" of each woman and man could be the place of such profound divisions.

The powerful words of Martin Luther King Jr. inspired a generation to work toward realizing his dream of a society where character mattered more than race, where inward truth outweighed outward appearances.

By King's courage and unwavering commitment to nonviolence, along with that of the many black and white citizens who participated in and supported the Civil Rights movement, today in the United States some aspects of this dream of unity are realized. This gives hope for those still struggling peacefully for justice.

Of course, the United States is not alone in being a place of dividedness and oppression of parts of the population. Most countries are home to a group of people that are ostracized and treated as lesser citizens, even lesser human beings. I am sure that you can come up with many examples yourself.

So let us listen and look around. Let us experience the dividedness of reality. And then let us see that we are not confined to this dividedness. We can grow! We can choose to walk across the street, to blur the line, and to step over the boundary in order to meet the other.

Jesus steps over many boundaries. He shares loaves and fishes with the poor on the hillside. He becomes friends with tax collectors. He even eats with Pharisees, the very people who are most suspicious of him. Astonishingly, "He said also to the man who had invited him, 'When you give a dinner or a banquet, do not invite your friends or your brothers or your kinsmen or rich neighbors, lest they also invite you in return, and you be repaid. But when you give a feast, invite the poor, the maimed, the lame, the blind, and you will be blessed, because they cannot repay you'" (Luke 14:12–14).

It is important to see that Jesus does not say that the people invited will be better off, but that "*you* [the well-off host] will be blessed." By sharing a table, by inviting those who are very different from us, those who are most rejected, we discover something beautiful. By facing our fears, by uncovering the walls of protection within us that keep us from even being able to look upon our brothers and sisters, the nature of our hearts begins to change. Not only is our human family beginning to be healed, but also our own hearts.

CHAPTER FOUR

Why Is There Evil in the World?

This is an excellent question. We must not live in a world of illusions or ideals. There is evil in the world—I have seen it, you have seen it. In this world, there are horrifying things that occur: murder, abuse, rape, genocide, torture. Greed is also evil, knocking down all these trees when we know that this will cause run-off, destroying the land, destroying harvests and causing people to suffer and die. Another example of greed is putting a barbed wire fence around an important water source so as to bottle it and sell it to faraway consumers. When we see evil, when we begin to touch it, it is so horrifying that we want to look away.

The twelfth and thirteenth chapter of the book of Revelation tell us about Satan, "a huge red dragon with seven heads and ten horns, and each of the seven heads crowned with a coronet" (Revelation 12:3, NJB). The chapter goes on to describe how "the dragon stopped in front of the woman as she was at the point of giving birth, so that it could eat the child as soon as it was born" (Revelation 12:4, NJB). The child is saved and the woman protected. There ensues an enormous battle and the dragon is "driven out of heaven. The dragon, the primeval serpent, known as the devil or Satan, who had led all the world astray, was hurled down to the earth and all his angels with him"

(Revelation 12:9, NJB). The story does not end there. The dragon continues to cause a ruckus and even is joined by a bizarre leopard beast that rises out of the sea.

What does it all mean? Can we say that evil originated by a rupture in heaven between God and his angels? I cannot say. Humanity has been looking into this question forever, but we never get satisfying answers. Wisdom is to be very humble. We don't know too much. But perhaps it does not matter. What I can say, and what you can say, is that evil exists.

Let us begin by looking at the world around us. I was visiting Honduras once, and a woman in our community there pointed out a house on a hillside. "It is the drug dealer's house," she said, "A gang seduces the young people by giving them drugs, by bringing them to the point of addiction. This drug-dealer is protected by the police, and the police are under the protection of the government." Looking at the house from the bottom of the hillside, it was easy to see what was happening. It was the death of youth, the enslavement of innocence, the destruction of those in whom there is every hope of growth to truth and love. Would you agree that this is evil?

We recognize evil because it is horrifying and repulsive. Just think about that image of a dragon about to eat a baby! It makes one want to cringe, to hide one's eyes and run in the other direction. Evil is the destruction or stamping out of life that is so repulsive that we want to run for protection before confronting it. Yet its curious power is that when we shield our eyes, cover our ears, and keep silent, we participate in it.

To collude with evil is to refuse to love and to resist the movement of life. When we begin to look, we may be astonished to find how prevalent this is and how unconsciously it occurs. We so easily get caught up in a desire to win, a desire to be the best, and a desire to succeed that we are willing to crush others. We become so focused upon a single goal that we lose sight of the primacy of truth and love. In a culture of normality defined by competition, mistrust, and greed, everybody loses.

Perhaps you have heard the story of Adam and Eve. The first chapters of the Bible describe how they were created and given a wonderful garden in which to live, a garden with trees of every kind, bearing all manner of delicious fruits and things to eat. God said to them, "You are free to eat of all the trees in the garden, but of the tree of the knowledge of good and evil you are not to eat; for, the day you are to eat of that, you are doomed to die" (Genesis 2:16–18, NJB).

You probably know what happens. Eve, encouraged by the serpent, takes some of the fruit. She shares the fruit with Adam. "Then the eyes of both of them were opened and they realized that they were naked" (Genesis 3:7, NJB). God comes to the garden searching, "Where are you?" "I was afraid because I was naked, so I hid," confesses Adam. "Who told you that you were naked?" asks God (see Genesis 3:9–11, NJB).

To face the reality of our humanity, we need a special source of life, we need grace, so as to live in and be part of God's kingdom. If we are to live with our nakedness—which is our human vulnerability—in God's garden, we must have the courage to say, "Here I am!" when God comes looking. We must open the doors of our hearts so that God may enter in and give us that strength.

What do you think? Are humans fundamentally sinful? What does that even mean?

My thought is that we are all broken people and that there is a tension within all of us. It manifests in moments when I am not really listening to someone, moments when I want to do my thing and not take time to be grateful for everything given, when I am not really listening to my conscience. Original or not so original, this struggle is within each of us. The important thing is to grow, to grow to greater love, to greater truthfulness, and to the audacity that witnesses to truth. The important thing is to heal those places of brokenness within each of us, to overcome the places of division, and to work through the barriers and the layers of protection.

So we cannot say where evil came from or *why* there is evil in the world. The important thing is to be aware that some kind of evil spirit does seem to exist. I don't mean that there is a devilish-looking fellow creeping about, ready to spring from under the stairs. I am talking about a way of being, about an evil that we all too easily become part of. It is all too easy to plant seeds of hatred, greed, and judgment. It happens quite unconsciously! When we are repulsed by evil to the point that we must turn away and pretend we never saw anything, we allow a division to form within us. How subtly evil works! In protecting ourselves, in turning away, in failing to witness to *life*, we become complicit.

Jesus describes how easily this can occur.

> When an unclean spirit goes out of someone, it wanders through waterless country looking for a place to rest, and not finding one, it says, "I will go back to the home I came from." But on arrival, finding it swept and put in order, it then goes off and brings seven other spirits more wicked than itself and they go in and set up house there, and so that person ends up worse off than before. (Luke 11:24–26, NJB)

It is a strong message. The "swept and tidied home" may be a person who assumes that she is rid of all possibility for evil. Her cleanliness may blind her to the presence of the unclean spirit and make her all the more vulnerable. You may have seen this happen. Sometimes it is the very people who seem to carry many qualities of leadership and altruism that blindly perpetuate divisions, create cliques, and turn away from or say nothing in the face of day-to-day injustices. Have you experienced these things?

On a bigger scale, we can see that even churches are not immune. Think of all the injustices to people with disabilities. Who is reacting against these? There are some issues that Church authorities have no trouble being very loud about. But it is not often that I hear them saying, "Go to the institutions, go to retirement homes, to the boarding houses, to the margins of society, and become their friends. Bring them into your communities, reveal to them how precious they are!" This is a question of justice, of freedom for our human family! And yet often the Church doesn't seem interested. They might congratulate L'Arche or a few people for being especially good because they are doing something about injustice. But it is not a matter of being good, it is about doing what is right. It is about fostering life rather than colluding with death.

The same Gospel text continues:

> It happened that as he was speaking, a woman raised her voice in the crowd and said, "Blessed the womb that bore you and the breasts that fed you!" But he replied, "More blessed still are those who hear the word of God and keep it!" (Luke 11:27–28, NJB)

We are never delivered from this possibility of evil. Even if our parents are wonderful people, even if we give birth to the most righteous of children, life is movement. It is a continuous journey of growth. And every step of the way, we can be open to life or we can participate in the crushing of it. We all have the possibility to "hear the word of God and keep it."

The first chapter of the Gospel of John helps us to see more clearly what might be implied by this "word of God." It is also a beautiful text.

In the beginning was the Word, and the Word was with God, and the Word was God. He was in the beginning with God; all things were made through him, and without him was not anything made that was made. In him was life, and the life was the light of all people. The light shines in the darkness, and the darkness has not overcome it. (John 1:1–5)

So the first observation is, the "Word of God" that we can "hear" and "keep" has something to do with fostering life: "All things were made through him.... In him was life." Whether or not we agree that God is behind all of this, we have seen evil, we have seen the destruction of life. We have seen that there are choices to be made that give life or crush it. We can be sucked into a world of competition, a world of ambitions and individual success. We can enter into the refusal of the Word. To keep the word must mean to choose life. And to choose life is to offer one's gifts for some greater purpose. It is to play a sport for the sake of the game and not for winning. It is to participate in theater because to represent something that is true is important, not because we have a need to be on stage. It is to play music because beauty can awaken people's hearts, not because we hope to be acclaimed.

The second observation is that the "light shines in the darkness, and the darkness has not overcome it." Life persists. It cannot be overcome. I have often marveled at little blades of grass that succeed in pushing up between concrete slabs on the sidewalk; at the persistence of butterflies who seem so fragile and migrate annually from Canada to Mexico; at the loyalty of geese who, while migrating, form a V to protect one another. And I am amazed by the little stories of community, of compassion, of unexpected love that come up in war zones and places of human catastrophe.

Life persists, even where it would seem impossible. Evil never dominates; "the darkness has not overcome it."

What does that mean in more everyday terms? It means that rather than seeking to destroy our enemies, rather than seeking to eliminate terrorists or shun multinational corporations, rather than fighting bullies or jailing delinquents, rather than judging Lazarus or blaming the rich man, we can pray that the light of goodness that exists in every human person may rise up.

Sometimes I read the news and I feel powerless. There are hundreds of people leaving home to join the radical militant groups every week. What can we even do in the face of such situations? How can peace ever be achieved? It is not clear what our role is in a conflict that in many ways is over and above us.

I was at a conference on the topic of seeing the goodness in each person and someone posed the question, "What about those jihadists, cutting off people's heads and everything?" The keynote speaker, Lytta Basset, looked at the group—primarily earnest Catholics—and asked, "Who here prays for the jihadists?" Not a single hand went up. Even in the face of such a feeling of powerlessness, we *can* do something. We can pray.

Praying implies that we take a moment to hold places of overwhelming conflict and injustice, to be there in spirit with the people whose names and faces we do not know but who are part of our one human family. Praying means that we create a special place in our hearts for those who are invaded by violence and cruelty, who are victims of deep fears and anguish. Praying means that even in our inability to take action, we prepare our hearts to welcome that little light of goodness and life that cannot be overcome, even in people who are violent. Praying means transforming our own hearts. It means asking Jesus for the strength and wisdom to love the way that he does—open and fearless.

This is what it means to grow in our humanity. It means to grow in our capacity to forgive and welcome those who seem so far from us, so difficult to love. This is essential to overcoming divisions. If a person is willing to cross the street near Santiago, it is because they believe that truth and love exist in some capacity on the other side. If Adam and Eve are to be reunited with God, it is because they believe in something within that is beautiful and precious. If the cycle of drug dealing and addiction is to come to an end, it is because the eyes of the dealers are opened up to the wonder and fragility of life and their responsibility to protect and foster it. It is by simple reverence and forgiving growth in love that evil is overcome.

CHAPTER FIVE

What Is the Nature of Reality?

Let us take a moment for review. We have observed the reality of terrific division in our world. We have also observed that divisions are the cause of enormous suffering. What then becomes evident is that as long as we remain locked in our own separate worlds, we cannot address divisions and suffering. We must seek to bring people together. We must visit nursing homes, volunteer at food banks and hospitals, and interest ourselves in unfamiliar traditions and religions. We must look to the back of the class if we sit at the front, and to the front of the class if we sit at the back. We must consider the chicken when we eat a drumstick and the fields when we eat a slice of bread. We must consider the implications of a dollar saved when we buy a generic chocolate bar rather than a fair trade one. We must not be satisfied with what is familiar or normal but look to expand our awareness of the world. We must live in reality.

What more can we say about reality? What is the *nature* of reality? Let us consider together. Reality is all that is. Because of this comprehensiveness, it is complex, it is tangible and intangible, it is physical and spiritual, and it is just beyond my own capacity to comprehend. It implies mystery: we are always learning more, becoming more open to reality and at the same time becoming aware of our littleness in it all. A friend used to say that knowledge is like an island in a sea of everything

I do not know. As I learn things, as I have new experiences, the island grows. But of course as the island grows, there is increasing contact with that sea of unknowing. In short, the more I know, the more I know I don't know.

Wisdom is to be very humble. I do not have the answers.

Reality is what we have heard, seen, watched, and touched. To live in reality, we must always be asking questions. Because something we can say about reality, something very important, is that it is shared. We can live in reality only if we are listening, if we are working to break down the barriers that separate us from one another. We can live in reality only if we are striving to overcome the divisions that make it so hard to hear what the other is saying. We need one another if we are to live in the fullness and complexity of reality.

Etty Hillesum wrote, "I shall no longer flirt with words, for words merely evoke misunderstandings."[3] We must be careful when verbalizing reality, for it is too complex for words. And yet, as we saw earlier when we were discussing suffering, we have a need to explain, to contextualize, to create structures within which we can form understanding. We need structures within which we can meet the other—a common space. When I say space, I do not mean just buildings. Structures include social spaces. They include ways of behaving that show our respect for others. When we enter a room, for example, how do we greet people? To whom do we turn? Structures even include temporal spaces; for example, we need a common concept of time to arrange a meeting by saying, "Let us meet at three this afternoon." And structures include language. What are the words that I can use to describe an experience so that we can share it in some way? In many subtle ways, we live within structures. In many ways, we are defined by structures.

I want to tell you a little story about structures of a very subtle nature.

Brenda is a wonderful woman who lives in my community. She doesn't speak very much, and when she does speak, it is in simple words or a sort of chatter that is quite incomprehensible. There are a few things, however, that she says quite often and they are now more easily identifiable. "Time is it?" is one of her favorite questions and one that easily gets an answer, which is probably why she likes it so much. In fact, her sense of time is pretty limited, so she is prone to asking this fifteen times in five minutes when she is feeling lonely or bored. Another question is, "When Annik?" Annik is her sister. Once a month Brenda spends a weekend with her sister, and she begins looking forward to the next time as soon as she gets back. Her third favorite phrase is a particular grace we sing before we eat; "Thank you, Alleluia." Again, it is very simple. She sings the first two notes, and then the whole table joins in.

For a long time when I was living with her, this is pretty much all that she would say: "Time is it?" "When Annik?" and "Thank you, Alleluia." When we had a prayer time in the evening, we would go around the circle and give everyone a chance to speak. "Brenda? Do you have something or someone to pray for?" She might sit silent for a moment or two, and so to help the situation, we might say, "For An—" "Annik, Annik!" she would finish off, as if she had just been waiting for our little leg up.

We could see that Brenda was living in a structure of understood phrases and words. It was wonderful in some ways because she had the bearings to be in contact with people around her. Her very structured vocabulary alleviated the suffering of not being able to dialogue. And we were alleviated of the suffering of feeling like we could not understand her.

One evening, the candle was lit, and we sat peacefully. People offered intentions and thanksgiving, mentioned names and future events, and shared experiences. When it was Brenda's turn, someone asked, "Bre, do you have a prayer?" She looked at the candle and then laughed. "Prayer," she chuckled. She said something that was not "Annik" or "Time" or "Thank you, Alleluia"! Then she said it again, "Prayer!" and laughed. This continued for several minutes. I wondered whether I should help her out of this apparent cycle by reminding her of her traditional prayer or with a definitive "Amen."

Then, with great composure, still focused on the candle, she said, "Thank you." And that was all. It was a wonderful reminder that Brenda does not exist within the cozy structure of habitual phrases. She is much more complex. Her experiences, her being, are beyond words. To come to know Brenda means to be continually surprised and opened up to the mystery of her being and therefore to our shared reality.

To grow, to expand our conception of reality, we must frequently be shaken from what I like to call our "cozy certitudes." We must be open to people whose experiences and perspectives are very different from our own. We must listen to them, take time with them, and hear the truth in their witness. This is why the *diversity* of humanity is vital. We can never say to someone who is of a different race, to someone who has a disability, to someone who seems a bit crazy, that they do not have an essential place in the human body. *Each of us* has an essential place.

Who are those people who destabilize us, who challenge our "cozy certitudes," who help us cross over the boundaries of even religious faith and go deeper into our shared experiences? Who are those people who help us to open up a little more to the fullness of reality?

I think that grandparents are such treasures. Often they are wonderful. I really mean this. Often they are full of wonder for their grandchildren and for their beautiful family. I remember someone saying that if he had known how much fun grandchildren were going to be, he would have had them first. Parents can be quite worried about their children, telling them what to do, trying to give advice and steer their children toward a successful adulthood. Grandparents are a different reality—dare I say, even a sacred reality. They seem to accept all, to forgive all. They are happy that their grandchildren simply exist!

And yet there is an enormous divide between our grandparents and us—greater than that between our parents and us. Our grandparents are elderly. They are not as quick as they once were. They may seem weak and foolish. They get tired easily and they forget names and dates. I know that I, at eighty-six, often forget words that once came to me quite readily. I have rediscovered something that I must have experienced as a little baby: there is a hiatus between the idea and the word. Sometimes I have a very clear image in my head, and yet the word is no longer there. Once I was giving a talk and describing that story that I shared with you about Santiago and the road between the rich side of town and the poor side of town. As I began speaking, I could see that the name of this city, which I had once pictured clearly, was gone! And as I approached the point in my talk where I usually said the name, I realized that I was going to have to come up with another way of expressing myself. So I said, "I was visiting a city in a country in South America…" and continued on.

Perhaps your grandmother has shared similar stories with you: times when she lost her glasses, only to find them on her head, or times when she forgot names from one minute to the next. It may seem to you like she is in a different world. And yet her reality and yours, however divided, is shared. Reality is shared between the very old and the very young, the ones who work and the ones who rest, the ones who are quick to rationalize and the ones who dare to dream. Without any of these, reality would not be complete.

Let us think again of Grandma. Perhaps she can do little but sit and hold your hand. And yet she is teaching you, helping you to experience things you never would experience on your own. Does she help you to be still? To listen? To take time with others? Do her words, even nonsensical, cause you to look at life a little differently? Does she smile a little broader when you are near? Does she sleep a bit more peacefully when you kiss her cheek good-bye? Without one another, your realities are not complete.

When we see that reality is shared, we must also see that listening is essential. We must learn to listen ever more deeply to those who open our eyes to a world that is unlike our own. What does listening mean?

Listening means to be opened up still further to the complexity of reality, to overcome divisions, to identify walls and break them down. It is not to say that we abandon ourselves; rather, we may come to know ourselves more deeply for being faced with difference.

In fact, if I am not firm in my sense of who I am, I may not be able to be open to the other because I will fear being lost or disoriented. Listening is about being open to modifications that bring me closer to the truth of our humanity, to the truth revealed in reality. Listening is to enter into unknown territory, which requires humility, but also the courage to say, "I don't know."

Listening is about understanding the need behind the communication. It implies greater purpose, greater attentiveness, and presence.

And yet when I listen, I do not try to possess you or assume what you are saying. I do not seek to judge or to condemn. I am simply receiving, accepting what you say, accepting all that you express, and accepting who you are. Listening implies deep respect and the conviction that the other is precious and has something important to express. Their experience of reality may not be my experience of reality, but it is just as authentic.

If we are listening, it means somewhere defense mechanisms have fallen down. There is no comparison. I am not trying to show that I am better. I am not preparing a rebuttal or a quick response. Listening implies vulnerability. Listening is about abandoning my own narratives and explanations. It is about abandoning structures and laws, and letting go of repairs. Listening implies abandonment and trust. It is a fundamental way of being that lets us live with openness to others. Listening is the way to live in reality because it is a way of life that is shared.

Of course, I am speaking about a way of being that is in a way *more* than listening. In French sometimes we use the word *bienveillance*. *Bien* means "good" and *veillance* means "surveillance" or "supervision." *Bienveillance*, then, is a way of welcoming and being with the other. It is the embodiment of the belief that the other is beautiful, wise, and fundamentally beloved, imbuing every physical contact, every regard, every motion of our body toward another, with the love and respect that we know they are worthy of. "Listening," then, is also way of looking that says, "You are precious and beautiful." It is a way of being that says, "I am happy that we are together."

Remember what I said about the island of knowledge growing in a sea of unknown? Notice that there is an island to begin with—a starting point, a point of departure. We know something. This is important. My experience is that when we live in a more complex reality, we quickly can feel destabilized. This is when we reach out for structures to contextualize and even protect us. But then we risk not living in reality. We risk creating division and perpetuating or participating in suffering. How are we to orient ourselves in the complexity that we must not deny?

I will propose something very simple. In living, we can always orient ourselves toward life.

CHAPTER SIX

What Are We Living For?

What *are* we living for? Are we living for our parents? Are we living for our teachers or for our friends or for a religious group? Are we living for our personal ambitions? Are we animated by compulsions?

Or are we living for truth? Are we living for justice? Are we living for freedom or happiness or hope or joy? Are we living for love? All of these are part of what it means to be living for life. Life is what ought to orient us in the contradictions, the paradox, and the complex fullness of reality. Is this the way that is life-giving, or is this the way that is life-impeding?

We discovered in the last chapter that if the nature of reality is shared, then we must learn to listen. Listening, remember, is about being open to modification, not trying to take control, but welcoming the other and welcoming life. Listening is about being attentive to the need behind the communication, the person behind the words, the fears behind the violence. Listening is about being attentive to the presence of life that cannot be overcome. Listening is about becoming vulnerable, about letting the defense mechanisms fall away that deafen us or influence what we take in. It is about humility before life, which is over and above us. Indeed, we can see that to be oriented toward life means to be listening.

We must be listening to the people around us with whom we share reality, especially to those people who seem to be very different from us, who challenge our experience of reality and expand it. We must be listening to elders whose years of experience have become wisdom. We must listen to the Word of God, to be challenged and affirmed by what we hear. We must listen to our Church, to the traditions and rules that have developed over two millennia. We must listen to the political, cultural, social, and environmental concerns that make up our historical context. In particular, we must listen to the little voice within us that orients us toward truth, toward love, toward justice, toward inner freedom, toward all these things that are complicit with life. This little voice is conscience.

Conscience is first of all an attraction, an attraction that is deep within us, guiding us to grow the way that a flower is attracted to the sun. It is feeling that we cannot quite explain, but that seems like coming home.

Perhaps one of my most significant experiences of conscience was in 1942 when I was thirteen years old. I had a deep sense that I should join the British Royal Navy. It was wartime. My father had participated in the war between 1914 and 1918. My older sister had gone to England and was part of the Canadian Women's Army Corps. So perhaps there was something there that had an influence on me. My brother once told me that I had seen a movie that had an effect of me. I have no recollection. All I know is that I had a very deep desire to go across the Atlantic from Canada to England and join the Royal Naval College.

I went to speak with my father. You can imagine his concern about his young son making such a dangerous journey. My family had had to leave my father's diplomatic posting because the Germans had invaded

France. We had come back to Canada in 1940. Here I was, only two years later, with an unshakable conviction that I must go back. He tried to offer different solutions. Perhaps I could wait a couple of years and go to Western Canada where there was a naval college for people a little older than I was at that time. But this was not what I wanted.

He could have forbidden me. He could have said that I was being foolish, that I did not know what was good for me. But he did not. He said something that in a way liberated me for my entire lifetime. He said, "I trust you. If that is what you want to do, then you should do it." He accepted that I needed to become free—free to follow my conscience, free to become myself.

Freedom does not come without responsibility. Now I had to prepare for and pass my entrance exams, leave behind a brother that I was very close to, and make my way alone to a future that I could not have known very much about. We cannot be reckless with the trust that people give us. Remember that listening to conscience is fundamental, but we must also be listening to the people around us and to the historical context in which we are called to live a response to conscience. In my case, it was clear that this was the right way forward. I passed my exams, I made it to London, and I found my place among the other young cadets. Eventually I made my way into the position of officer, transferring to the Canadian Navy. In many ways, my career in the military was a success.

But after eight years, I had a very deep sense that I should leave the military. I can now say that this was another occasion of conscience. There was an attraction within me that I needed to respond to, something more fundamental than my parents' desires or the navy's expectations or the approval that I was receiving from others for my service. It was a growing need to go to worship, to spend time in prayer, to read books and contemplate. At one point I visited "Friendship House" in New York and celebrated Thanksgiving with the poor people there. It was a wonderful experience, one of happiness and the feeling of being home. It was a confirmation of this growing attraction to the religious sphere rather than the military sphere. So after a time of accompanied discernment, I resigned from the navy.

Conscience is something that echoes deep inside of us and helps us live in harmony and grow to greater love, truth, and inner freedom. It calls us to grow to a plenitude of our humanity; it calls us to grow to God. The first chapter of *Gaudium et Spes* (which means Joy and Hope), a text resulting from the Second Vatican Council, describes the dignity of the human person.

> Conscience is the most secret core and sanctuary of a human being. There one is alone with God, Whose voice echoes in one's depths. In a wonderful manner, conscience reveals that law which is fulfilled by love of God and neighbor.[4]

Each of us is born with a particular and unique genetic makeup. This determines how long our nose will be, what color our hair or eyes might be, the size of our feet, and so on. Our physical genes help us to grow. We also have this other impulse to grow, something like "spiritual genes" that help us to grow in our humanity. But conscience, this little voice that calls us to live and to speak truth, can easily be stifled or manipulated.

In life we face pressures from all sides—expectations of our society, of our culture, of our community, and of our friends. Sometimes we confuse the voice of conscience with the voice and desires of our parents. When we are very young, we trust our parents and tend to listen to them. After all, they want us to grow, and with their greater amount of life experience, they can help us a lot. But then there comes a certain age where we may realize that parents make mistakes. We may realize that what my parents want me to do, what they desire for my life, does not correspond with what I desire for my life. This can put us into a spirit of rebellion, rejecting everything that our parents suggest to us.

Perhaps you can see the irony in this. So long as we are simply rebelling, our parents still control what we do. To live in rejection of something is nevertheless to be governed by it, to be living in response to what we are rebelling against. Does that make sense? Somehow we must become free to live in response to our conscience. Sometimes this means doing things that make our parents happy and sometimes not. Sometimes this means doing what we might think of as "cool" and sometimes not.

The birth of conscience may come with the discovery that I am somebody. I am not my mother, I am not my father, I am not my best friends, and I am not my teacher. I am unique and with my own impulse to grow, my own capacity to know what is right and what is wrong, what is good and what is evil, what leads to growth and what does not. We can see in my own story that there was something of this when I went to my father and told him of my project to go to England. There is something of a conversion when I do something I *know* is right, even though others are opposed to it. But it is so difficult! Our parents tell us not to take drugs. Is there a birth of conscience when we go against this advice? We must look more deeply into the question. Why would we take drugs? Is it the right thing to do? Or is it the thing that all of our friends do? Or perhaps it is a way of hiding or running away from reality? In that case we have not made a choice in freedom. There is no sense of "I am"—I am someone free, I am a source of life, and I am a wellspring of peace.

I was interested to read that today's younger generation is sometimes referred to as the "Me Generation." What is the difference between "me" and "I am"? For one thing, *me* is passive. "A friend sent a package to me." "The music surrounded me." "You went on ahead without me." *I am* implies action, ownership, and responsibility. "I am choosing…" "I am happy…" "I am growing…" "I am furious…" "I am sorry…" "I am with you."

There is something important about "I am" in the Bible as well. In the third chapter of the book of Exodus, God appears to Moses in a burning bush. God asks Moses to free the Israelites from their oppression in Egypt. "Moses then said to God, 'Look, if I go to the Israelites and say to them, 'The God of your ancestors has sent me to you,' and they say, 'What is his name?', what am I to tell them?' God said to Moses, 'I am who is.' And God said, 'This is what you are to say to the Israelites, 'I am has sent me to you'" (Exodus 3:13–14, NJB).

When a sense of "I am" is born within us, we can see that we have become aware of the presence of God within us.

We must learn to come back to this realization of Bonhoeffer's: God knows us. *I am Thine*, I am God's beloved. We must learn to listen to the presence of God within us—our conscience. There are many ways to do this. Etty Hillesum said we need half an hour of gymnastics and half an hour of silence each day. We need space and silence, we need time to be present to ourselves, to our desires, and time to be present to our bodies. We must learn to spend time in that inner sanctuary where God's voice resonates, leading us to the fulfillment of our humanity. Often it is good to have the accompaniment of someone wise, someone who knows us and who can teach us something about spiritual discipline. The important thing is that conscience never takes us out of reality but orients us within it. Conscience is the deepest secret of our vitality.

CHAPTER SEVEN

Why Is It So Hard to Be Good?

For many, to be good is to obey parents, teachers, religious structures, and so on. In fact, goodness is lived in little ways, loving those around us daringly and with compassion. To be good is to be a small wellspring of life. So let us rephrase the question. Evil is subtle, and it is easy to become complicit in the destruction of life. Rather than asking ourselves, "Why is it so hard to be good?" let us inquire, "What inhibits me from being open to life?"

Remember that being oriented toward life implies a sort of listening. We must listen to those around us with whom we share reality, those who have lengthier or different experiences from our own, those who are wise and want to teach us. We must listen to the world around us in the sense that we are given to live in a unique historical moment. And we must be listening to that little voice within us, the attraction to truth and love, that guides our human growth. When we are listening on these three levels, we can live in such a way that we are open to the movement of life. So the question, "What inhibits me from being open to life?" might become, "What inhibits me from listening?"

Let us speak again of barriers. There are divisions within us that are barriers to listening. Do you remember that story of the drug dealer? I saw his house in Honduras on the hillside, and I was told that he seduced young people into becoming addicts, and that he was protected by the police and government. What are the barriers that make it so difficult for anyone to hear the cry of young people whose lives become manipulated and crushed? Let us look at the situation carefully. There is evil activity: youths whose lives become enslaved by addiction. This reality is divided by a complex structure of responsibility that shields each of those participating—the members of the drug dealing gang, the police, the government, perhaps even the locals—from the atrocity of what is happening. Perhaps there is less outright violence, fewer clashes in the street. The violence may be subtler in nature and more easily ignored.

With the diffusion of reality, a comfortable atmosphere of apathy is created so that corruption can thrive. Apathy is about going along with everyone else and numbing the feeling that there is something terribly wrong. Our conscience cries out against corruption, but apathy stifles that cry. When our conscience is stifled, the life within *us* is stifled. When this occurs within us, we may feel a sense of powerlessness. We do not know who we are anymore; we do not know which way to turn or how to grow. Our deepest identity is stifled. This is anguish.

Anguish is one of those words that is not very easy to define, but all of us have experienced anguish in our bodies. Anguish has been described as the feeling of standing on the edge of a precipice and looking down. Have you ever been to the Grand Canyon or stood somewhere a bit precarious? It can be something like an experience of death and powerlessness, a reminder of the reality that our own way of growth is uncertain.

What is the difference between anguish and fear? We fear something outside of us: a dog that is barking loudly, a car that comes screeching to a halt as we are on the crosswalk, the feeling that someone is lurking in the dark just around the corner or behind the closed door. Fear is a barrier, a wall of protection or a defense mechanism that comes up when we feel vulnerable. We may fear the judgment of others when we take a risk or do something new. We fear humiliation.

Here we come very close to the distinction between anguish and fear. Humiliation is anguish, for it implies a loss of sense of self. We suffer it deeply. I sometimes think that we fear humiliation more than we fear anything else. Have you ever been humiliated? When anguish begins to rise up, we seek to protect ourselves in the same way that we try to protect ourselves from a dog, creating defense mechanisms. We have a fear of anguish.

And yet anguish is within each of us. Let me tell a little story. A father spoke to me not long after the birth of his second child. He described his daughter screaming at him a few days after her little brother came home. "I hate you, I hate you, I hate you!" she said. "I saw in her eyes," the father told me, "that she really meant it." Anguish is the deep suffering of losing one's place, of being betrayed by those closest to you and no longer knowing who you are, of being stripped in some way of the construction of our identity. Anguish is existential suffering; I do not know who I am.

That is the big question. Who are we? We know that something of our deepest identity is conscience, guiding us toward growth in justice and peace, in truth and in love. If we are to *grow* in truth and in love, then something of our deepest identity must be of truth and love. There is within us a treasure of truth and love, the treasure of our humanity. We might call this our belovedness.

What do I mean by belovedness? I mean that as human beings, we are endowed with love. Each of us has a heart to love others, a heart that is worthy of love in return. Some people have been so wounded, it is hard to perceive this, but do you think that there is anyone for whom it is not true? Each of us was carefully held in a womb, a precious miracle of life. And each of us, when we were born, reached out to hold and to be held. To be human is to love and to be loved. We are *fundamentally beloved.*

Belovedness, our deepest identity, is realized—meaning made real— in relationship. This seems obvious, but it is very important to make clear. We cannot be loved and we cannot love if we are all alone. This makes belovedness quite fragile. We depend upon others to realize who we are. Anguish is utter aloneness. When our love for someone is not accepted, when we ourselves are rejected, we experience a terrible suffering.

It is interesting to bring these things back to the child and the mother. Of course this may not be your experience. Some of us were deeply wounded in these early days and carry a deep anguish. Healing will come through another relationship that reveals to us our belovedness. But for many, this begins with the relationship between child and mother. After the shock, traumatic and glorious, of your birth, your mother and then your father held you warmly and securely. Through their physical presence and by your own body's response, you knew that you were beloved. The relationship between a parent and child is something beautiful. It is tender, it is touch, and it is playfulness. It is sensed through the body—through the look that says, "You are beautiful," the embrace that says, "You are precious," the listening that says, "You have something important to share."

The role of the body is so essential. Too often we can become intellectual about topics like conscience, God, even love. But the amazing mystery of Jesus is that "the Word became flesh and dwelt among us"

(John 1:14). God's love is made known to us in the flesh, in our bodies. And this begins from the time of our infancy. And yet there is something fearful in this, because the body of the child is in movement. He doesn't know where he is growing to, and so there is anguish: Will I always be loved? This does not destroy the joy of being together, but because of the intrinsic biological movement, because of the impulse to grow that is within each of us, there is uncertainty. Who am I becoming?

Let's think about that older sister with her new baby brother. Imagine her insecurity. Before her brother came along, she had all the love of her parents. Now it is being shared. Was she not good enough? Had she done something wrong? Guilt and anguish are very closely related. She may have felt that she now had to prove that she was still lovable, to prove that she was still someone who her parents wanted. She had in some way lost her identity of belovedness.

When we, as young children, begin to leave the embrace of our mother—when another child comes and takes our place or we begin to realize that our parents' lives do not revolve solely around us— anguish rises up very quickly. If we are not grounded in our belovedness of God as the heart of our lives, we will look to be loved for the things that we do. Quickly we enter into a culture of proving ourselves, a culture of seeking applause and admiration, a culture of fear should we be rejected, and a culture of normality. We need to somehow recover that knowledge that we are fundamentally beloved. We need to discover another embrace, the embrace of God who holds us unconditionally and whose capacity is infinite. For Christians, this is baptism. Essentially, it is about rebirth, the revelation of our identity of belovedness, which means that even before belonging to our family, we belong to God. To know this implies a grace of God. An identity of beloved-ness brings us to union in love with the whole of the human family. It brings us so near to God that our heart opens up to all that God loves.

To come back to our initial question, perhaps we can say that it is not hard to be good. It is not hard to be open to life, to grow, so long as we are listening to conscience. But conscience is stifled by our fears, by that profound system of protection within us.

When have you failed to be good? When have you not been able to listen? Maybe there was a time when someone said something cruel, and you laughed without thinking about it. Maybe someone you find really annoying asked for your help, but you said that you were too busy to help. Maybe you even listened to an unkind rumor and did not point out that it was hurtful and untrue. There are so many little ways in which we participate, even naïvely, in the suffering of others. If we dig a little deeper into each of these scenarios, we will discover that fear truly does lie at the root. We laugh first because of a deep fear that we ourselves might be laughed at. We don't take the time for others because we have a fear that we might fail. We don't insist upon the truth because we have a fear of being ridiculed ourselves.

Little by little we can begin to name our fears, we can begin to work at taking them down one by one. But sometimes we seem to get to a closed door. There is no one who knows us through and through. Each person who tells us that they love us knows us to a certain extent, but each of has our secrets. And so we have a profound loneliness; we have anguish. The question is, "When will that door be opened? When will we be freed from our anguish? When will we be free to love? When will we know that we are fundamentally beloved?"

In the first chapter of the book of Jeremiah, God says, "Before I formed you in the womb I knew you; before you came to birth I consecrated you; I appointed you as a prophet to the nations" (Jeremiah 1:5, NJB). Perhaps the solution to our anguish has something to do with the one who created us, the one who knows us more intimately than anyone else can.

But does God actually exist?

CHAPTER EIGHT

How Do You Know That God Exists?

If you ask me personally, I would say that I know God exists because I grew up in a family where it was just evident, where faith was part of my life. We would say prayers at night before going to bed, we would go to Eucharist, and so on. Our faith was just part of every day. So it was obvious. Of course, even though I was brought up believing in God, there has been a great change in me as well. I am no longer as I was when I was in my family, and so my relationship with God has been an evolving one. That is life.

Today I meet with people who say that they are atheist, people who don't believe in God. Here again we are faced with the dividedness of our reality. For me, God is present in everything I do. God even is present for me in everything that *they* do, even when they do not see this themselves! They simply don't have the same experience as I do. It is as if we had gone for a long walk together, but afterward I insisted that we had walked through a forest while they were sure that we had been in a grassy field. So the question is, "How can we meet? How can we live in our shared reality?"

I say to the atheist: "There is one thing that I know. Love is better than hate. That I *know*. Because I have seen the fruits of hate, of people killing each other, stealing from one another, oppressing and humiliating one another. I have been to prisons and met with youth whose lives have been crushed by those who refused to give them an ounce of respect. I have visited people who have built thick walls of protection and become tough gangsters. I have seen all of this. And what is clear is that love is better than hate."

So even before we enter a discussion of whether God exists, we can discover the fundamental thing: that love and hate exist. How is it that some people—including people of faith—can be locked up in ideas? They may believe in God, but they do not seem to know love. How is it that they can continue to live in a world of ideas which seems to make them incapable of listening to people who are different?

Perhaps we must look a little more closely at what hate is.

Hate has diverse forms. There is a visible hate and an invisible hate. Visible hate is pretty obvious. It is bullying, violence, abuse, and so on. We catch glimpses of hate every day when we see terrible headlines in news reports. We sometimes encounter hate in our communities, our workplaces, and our schools when we hear racist or sexist comments, or when someone in our group is excluded.

Invisible hate is more subtle but perhaps more rampant. It is someone cutting down all the trees and refusing to see the effects of their destruction. It is promoting anti-immigration policies that turn residents against those who are new in their country. Greed and egoism can be a form of hate too. In the rich man, across the street from Lazarus, there is a form of hate. It is not a visible hate; he is not going to go to the other side of the road and give a kick to Lazarus. But somewhere in him, there is a hate. Somewhere he hasn't accepted that huge secret, which is not so secret, that we are all part of the human family.

Whether we are rich or poor, Russian or Ukrainian, young or old, Hutu or Tutsi, we are all part of the same human family. And yet we have within us the capacity to refuse to speak with someone, to avoid sitting next to them at the table, to block ourselves off from contact with any person we have difficulties with. These separations are invisible hate because we do not accept the existence of the other, we do not accept our shared reality. Hatred means that somewhere in our life we are afraid of crossing the road.

The correlation between fear and hatred should be pretty evident, particularly today as anti-Islamic sentiment is growing rapidly due to terrorist activity. In Canada, while I have been writing this, a young Muslim man shot and killed a member of the military. Of course it is tragic and people were quite shaken. How does a country respond to such an act? The Prime Minister's response was a reassertion of the country's commitment to fight terrorism on an international level. Security measures across the country were raised, particularly at various government locations and military bases. "Canada will never be intimidated," he emphasized.

But what is actually the most *courageous* response to an act of terrorism? What if Canada had responded by calling upon every citizen to reach out to those on the peripheries of our society: those who are the loneliest, those who feel rejected and fearful, and those who are the most at risk of becoming extremists?

Etty Hillesum writes that she "see[s] no alternative: each of us must turn inward and destroy in himself all that he thinks he ought to destroy in others. And remember that every atom of hate we add to this world makes it all the more inhospitable."[5]

Atoms of hate, as we can see, are fears—fears so well-installed that by the time they become hatred, it is not immediately obvious that the young man who was drawn into terrorism was fearful. In the last chapter we looked at our own occasions of failing to do good, and we explored the fears that motivate us, however subtly. In a similar way, we can look into the story of a young terrorist and into the story of others who are caught in a web of hate, which is to be caught in a web of fear.

I like to tell the story of a man who was in the mafia. He grew up in a very tough atmosphere, one of violence, drugs, and power struggles for survival. When he was young, no one told him, "I love you and you are beautiful." He had never learned to trust another human being. Instead he had learned that people are mean and that to stay alive he had to become stronger than the next guy. And so his fear of being knocked down, of being the weakest, grew into hatred. Even as a child, he protected himself with violence, manipulation, hiding, and destroying. As he grew older, he thought that no one would ever help him. And in a way it was true. So long as he was very strong, it was difficult to come close to him. His fear had created hard systems of protection that made others afraid of him. The struggle to survive is lonely. How does the fear cycle, this germination of hatred, come to an end? It has something to do with becoming weak and vulnerable. Let us continue with the story of the mafia man to see how this can be true.

Many years later, the mafia man was in prison and dying of cancer. A friend of mine is a doctor who treats prison inmates, and he was called in to treat him. The mafia man had a very painful kind of throat cancer. He was weak when my friend met him. He was helpless. Perhaps he was afraid to have my friend come close to him at first. But he had no choice except to face his fears. He had to accept my friend's help; he had to trust him. Perhaps my friend was a little apprehensive himself when he first approached this criminal, this tough man. But he had no choice either. And my friend was gentle, touching the places where the mafia man needed healing with tenderness. In a beautiful way, the man's weakness brought them together and helped them overcome their fears. Gradually they became good friends, discovering that the other is not someone to be feared, but someone to laugh with, someone to talk with, someone to look forward to seeing. It was in a space of vulnerability, vulnerability and relationship in the body, that love was revealed.

We have looked at hate. We have seen that hate and fear are very, very close to one another. They are walls that barricade our hearts. We have begun to talk about love, to see that love begins with weakness. There is a beautiful text from Ezekiel where God promises that our "hearts of stone" will be replaced with "hearts of flesh" (Ezekiel 36:26, NJB). A heart of flesh is much more easily wounded. It is vulnerable. And yet a heart of flesh is a human heart, one capable of love. Learning to love has something to do with becoming more and more vulnerable, transforming my heart from one that is hard and cold to one that is tender and warm.

Now we have seen that love is better than hate, let us take time to see what it means to love. This may lead us back to the question of God.

CHAPTER NINE

How Can We Love?

In the tenth chapter of the Gospel of Luke, a lawyer tests Jesus by asking him, "What shall I do to inherit eternal life?" Jesus reminds him of the Law, which the lawyer is clearly familiar with, "You shall love the Lord your God with all your heart, and with all your soul, and with all your strength, and with all your mind; and your neighbor as yourself" (Luke 10:25, 27). The lawyer asks who is his neighbor, and Jesus tells him the story of the Good Samaritan.

> A man was going down from Jerusalem to Jericho, and he fell among robbers, who stripped him and beat him, and departed, leaving him half dead. Now by chance a priest was going down that road; and when he saw him, he passed by on the other side. So likewise a Levite, when he came to the place and saw him, passed by on the other side. But a Samaritan, as he journeyed, came to where he was; and when he saw him, he had compassion, and went to him and bound up his wounds, pouring on oil and wine; then he set him on his own beast and brought him to an inn, and took care of him. (Luke 10:30–34)

The parable reveals that we do not choose our neighbors. But we must love them.

St. Thérèse de Lisieux tells of a sister in her community that she had to work with. She found her absolutely disagreeable and to work side by side with her made Thérèse want to run away. If it made her want to run, it is because being near this woman brought up such an anguish that Thérèse had to protect herself. Have you had such an experience yourself? I am sure that there are people that you try to avoid in the hallways, people that you hope will not be in your classroom or work group. There may even be people you find unbearable. We would never have chosen them to be our neighbor. And so the question isn't "Who is our neighbor?" It is "How can we love?"

What can we say about love? I think we can say that it begins with an attraction. How did you meet your friends? Sometimes it is hard to remember. Many of my friendships have begun in L'Arche, beginning with some common interests. Are you part of any groups at that meet regularly because you share an interest, a hobby, or are working together on a project? Sometimes we discover that the project is just an excuse to be together; we simply enjoy one another's company. We enjoy being together; it makes us happy, a feeling that is physical, in our bodies. Friendship is about attraction and about growing into a relationship.

But what about a relationship with people that we would never think to speak with, people we are not at all attracted to? What about people who are very different from us? Sometimes we are attracted to someone who seems to need our help. Once, when I was visiting Lourdes, I was drawn to a man who was begging everyday not far from my hotel. He looked a little bit cold and quite poor, so I brought him coffee in the morning. It seemed to do him good.

The Gospel of John tells us a story about an encounter a little bit like this one, one where need or weakness brings people together.

Jesus, wearied as he was with his journey, sat down beside the well. It was about the sixth hour. There came a woman of Samaria to draw water. Jesus said to her, "Give me a drink." For his disciples had gone away into the city to buy food. The Samaritan woman said to him, "How is it that you, a Jew, ask a drink of me, a woman of Samaria?" For Jews have no dealings with Samaritans. Jesus answered her, "If you knew the gift of God, and who it is that is saying to you, 'Give me a drink,' you would have asked him, and he would have given you living water." (John 4:6–10)

Just as it is unlikely that I would spend time with a beggar outside my hotel in Lourdes, it was a bit unlikely that Jesus would spend time with this woman. In fact, if we look closely, there are three ways in which Jesus and this woman are quite divided from one another, three divisions that make this encounter remarkable.

The first division, carefully pointed out by the author, is the religious difference that had created great animosity between Jews and Samaritans. Both groups were descendants of Abraham, but the Samaritans lived in the Northern Kingdom of Israel. At some point, they were occupied by the Assyrians, and so their religious practice developed quite differently from the Jewish people. They believed in the first five books of Scripture, but not in the books of the prophets nor the books of wisdom. They also had a different place of worship. The Jewish people worshipped in the Temple in Jerusalem. The Samaritans worshipped on Mount Gerizim. As they are speaking, the woman asks about this.

"Our fathers worshiped on this mountain; and you say that in Jerusalem is the place where [people] ought to worship." Jesus said to her, "Woman, believe me, the hour is coming when neither on this mountain nor in Jerusalem will you worship the Father…. But the hour is coming, and now is, when the true worshipers will worship the Father in spirit and truth, for such the Father seeks to worship him. God is spirit, and those who worship him must worship in spirit and truth." (John 4:20–24)

Jesus does not entertain the division between them but affirms that all who are committed to the truth, all who are committed to God, are "true worshippers."

A second division is quite subtly indicated. This woman is filling up her jars at midday. Why would a woman fill up her jars in the middle of the day when the sun is at its highest point and the walk to and from her home is the most unbearable? All the other women fill up their jars when it is cool. They go together, talking among themselves. This woman, it would seem, wants to avoid the others. The heat of the sun is less painful than the humiliation of being around them. Why is she so disrespected and ashamed? We find out when Jesus says, "You are right in saying, 'I have no husband'; for you have had five husbands, and he whom you now have is not your husband; this you said truly" (John 4:17–18). And so Jesus is not only conversing with a Samaritan, but one whose sexual relationships would make her ostracized in any community where she was living, Samaritan or Jewish.

A third division is quite obvious. Jesus is a man and she is a woman. It is clear that in those days (as today in many parts of the world), men and women did not speak freely with one another. The text says that when the disciples come later, they "marveled that he was talking with a woman" (John 4:27) But they do not question him. By this time they are probably used to Jesus's insistence upon meeting people that one wouldn't expect.

Returning to the beggar I encountered at Lourdes, I enjoyed spending a bit of time with him. I brought him coffee several times, and we began having little conversations, enjoying also one another's presence without words, being with one another through the body. On the last day that I was there, I asked him where he had slept the night before. "Oh, just in a little hotel not too far from here." He explained that the price was very reasonable and that he wasn't planning on staying in Lourdes too much longer anyhow. You see, he had a little apartment in another city but he didn't have a refrigerator. And so he had come to beg for enough money to buy one. Once he had enough, he would go back home. I must admit, I was a bit surprised and amused at the irony of this apparent false beggar.

Perhaps the woman at the well felt a little bit like I did when, after Jesus had asked *her* for a drink, he says to her, "If you knew the gift of God, and who it is that is saying to you, 'Give me a drink,' you would have asked him, and he would have given you living water" (John 4:10). I did not remind the beggar that *he* was the one sitting on a sidewalk with an empty hat in front of him. I did not point out that *I* was the one who had been bringing him coffees because *he* looked cold and too poor to buy his own. The woman at the well was bolder and indicated to Jesus the irony of his claim. "Sir, you have nothing to draw with, and the well is deep; where do you get that living water? Are you greater than our father Jacob, who gave us the well, and drank from it himself, and his sons, and his cattle?" (John 4:11–12)

Jesus does not answer the question directly. "Every one who drinks of this water will thirst again, but whoever drinks of the water that I shall give him will never thirst; the water that I shall give him will become in him a spring of water welling up to eternal life" (John 4:13–14). This water is in response to a deeper thirst, one that the woman is not even immediately aware of. Jesus is about to reveal the weakness of our belovedness, which is our human need for one another.

The woman still isn't sure what he is talking about. But the water sounds like it would save her a lot of work. "'Sir, give me this water, that I may not thirst, nor come here to draw.' Jesus said to her, 'Go, call your husband, and come here.' The woman answered him, 'I have no husband.' Jesus said to her, 'You are right in saying, "I have no husband"'" (John 4:15–17). Jesus reveals to her her deepest thirst, which is her loneliness. She has lived only broken relationships, she goes to the well alone because she cannot be with the others in her village. The answer to her question, "Where do you get that living water?" is simple, and it is already being answered. It has nothing to do with a bucket, it is simply by being together, spending time in one another's company. It is love that Jesus is offering, that Jesus is giving. It is love that will quench her human thirst and that will transform her into someone who is able to love others in return, becoming "a spring of water welling up to eternal life."

I remember a city where overnight, most of the street people replaced their signs asking money for a sign that said, "A smile please!" Too often we turn our heads when we see someone begging on the street, shying away from looking into their eyes as we say that we haven't any change. And yet, what are they begging for? I have been to food banks and soup kitchens in North America that are overflowing with day-old baked goods. Bread satisfies a secondary hunger. Spare change is like well water. What about that water which is the meeting of eyes that says, "You are a human being."

When Jesus's disciples come back, they urge him to eat something.

> "Rabbi, eat." But he said to them, "I have food to eat of which
> you do not know.... My food is to do the will of him who sent
> me, and to accomplish his work.... I tell you, lift up your eyes,
> and see how the fields are already white for harvest. He who
> reaps receives wages, and gathers fruit for eternal life, so that
> sower and reaper may rejoice together." (John 4:31–36)

Love allows us to rejoice together. It is about the revelation of the value
and beauty of the person behind the function, behind his "different-
ness," behind his brokenness or strangeness. We are no longer sowers
and reapers but people, hungry and sharing our harvest. We are no
longer beggars and donors, we are no longer Samaritans and Jews, we
are no longer simply the role that we fulfill or the function that we
serve. Love reveals that we are all human beings. Perhaps I thought
that I was going to do good to this beggar by giving him coffee.
Perhaps the woman at the well thought that she was going to do good
to this tired traveler by fetching him water. But then with love comes
the astonishing revelation that we are all thirsty for relationship. And
when we come together, we discover living water. I was nourished by
my exchanges with the beggar in Lourdes, by the exchanged words and
laughter, by a feeling of friendliness. And he too was fortified, not by
the coffee (in fact I am sure that they had cheap coffee in his hotel),
but by the time I took to be with him, by the moments of sitting on the
pavement, both of us sharing and receiving.

How can we love? Perhaps we begin by daring to open our hearts to
those around us, especially with those whom we are a little afraid of
being in relationship. There are some people we cannot stand, some

people who, like Thérèse de Lisieux describes, make us want to run away. To run away in that sense is to reinforce the walls of fear that protect us from the anguish that the other seems to bring up in us. We can never begin to address this anguish unless we are willing to face our fears.

Thérèse decided that every time she had to be with that sister, she would give her most beautiful smile. When we dare, things happen. Just as I described how love reveals the person behind the function, so too can we discover the person behind the annoying traits, the beautiful human being that seems to be hidden behind all that makes us want to run. After a time, the woman asked her, "Thérèse, why is it that you seem to like me so much?" Love is hard work sometimes, but it is always possible.

Growth begins when I can say, "There is a brokenness within me. With some people, I can be open, at ease and welcoming. But with others, I can become closed off and mean. I find myself unable to trust them, and there is something that makes me want to turn away." Growth can only begin when I dare to ask myself why that is. And in asking myself, "why," I begin to dismantle the system of protection within me. I learn to accept that underneath all of those barriers, I am vulnerable and weak. There is a struggle, even in the reality of my own body. Perhaps I know that you are precious, but I am unable to look at you and see that; I am unable to imbue the touch of my hand with respect for you as a human person. Somewhere I am not confident in my own humanity. I need you. In some mysterious way, we are united in one human family. But the uncertainty of it all raises anguish. It is only when we dare to accept this anguish that we can begin to love.

CHAPTER TEN

How Can We Be of Service to One Another and to the World?

"And so, my fellow Americans: ask not what your country can do for you—ask what you can do for your country. My fellow citizens of the world: ask not what America will do for you, but what together we can do for the freedom of man [and woman]"⁶

When we begin to love, when we begin to see the beauty of every person, there arises in us a desire to change the world. We begin to see the systems in place that institutionalize injustice. Why don't politicians do something? How do we allow financial markets more influence than citizens? Food banks do not seem to do enough. The poor man on the street symbolizes a greater societal need for policy changes, for more creative assistance programs, for a radical change in the mainstream cultural mindset and in our approach to what it means to be human.

One of my students was very active during high school. She and some of her friends had a group that would meet weekly to discuss world issues, hosting debates among the students on such issues as the ethics of consumerism, the effectiveness of different voting systems, and whether violence is ever acceptable as a resolution to conflict. They raised money for schools in poor countries recognizing that it is in the interest of students today that their peers around the globe receive an education so as to participate fully in the global challenges that face their generation.

After graduating from high school, she decided to study economics so that eventually she would be able to design policy and affect *real* change in the world. It seemed to her that riding her bike or volunteering a couple of hours a week at a homeless shelter was hardly a drop in the bucket when it came to addressing the bigger issues such as climate change and homelessness. What is needed, she concluded, is a voice in the upper echelons of decision-making that speaks on behalf of those who are so often kept silent.

Our world needs people who are able to take the message of those on the streets into government buildings and investment centers. Our world needs people like Aung San Suu Kyi, a member of the Burmese parliament and head of the National League for Democracy in Burma. Although her party won 59 percent of the popular vote and 81 percent of the seats in parliament in 1990, she was kept under house arrest for fifteen of the following twenty-one years. But her dream and commitment to democracy and to nonviolence in her country could not be detained. She received enormous international recognition, including the Nobel Peace Prize in 1991. In 2010 she was released, and in 2012 she was elected to parliament in national by-elections. Her speech, "Freedom from Fear" (1990) is both visionary and an insightful commentary about the realty of politics in Burma and the rest of the world. It begins, "It is not power that corrupts but fear. Fear of losing power corrupts those who wield it and fear of the scourge of power corrupts those who are subject to it.... With so close a relationship between fear and corruption it is little wonder that in any society where fear is rife corruption in all forms becomes deeply entrenched."[7]

She is one of many who have found themselves in places of leadership with an agenda of justice and freedom. Others include William Wilberforce, Nelson Mandela, Vandana Shiva, and Malala Yousafzai. Many leaders are lesser known but work tirelessly to affect high levels of decision-making. Theirs is a thankless job, prone to enormous criticism from all sides but so important to furthering the work of peace in the world.

So how can we be of service to one another and to the world? There is a young man who asks a similar question of Jesus in the nineteenth chapter of the Gospel of Matthew.

> And behold, one came up to him, saying, "Teacher, what good deed must I do, to have eternal life?" And he said to him, "Why do you ask me about what is good? One there is who is good. If you would enter life, keep the commandments." He said to him, "Which?" And Jesus said, "You shall not kill, You shall not commit adultery, You shall not steal, You shall not bear false witness, Honor your father and mother, and, You shall love your neighbor as yourself." The young man said to him, "All these I have observed; what do I still lack?" Jesus said to him, "If you would be perfect, go, sell what you possess and give to the poor, and you will have treasure in heaven; and come, follow me." When the young man heard this he went away sorrowful; for he had great possessions. (Matthew 19:16–22)

I wonder which was actually the most difficult for the young man to hear: "Sell what you possess and give to the poor" or "Come, follow me." The first is already a pretty big challenge. If this is what made the young man turn away, maybe he had a sense that he was not doing everything he could to "love your neighbor as yourself." Perhaps he thought of someone like Lazarus and wondered, "Is this man his neighbor?" But what might have been even more difficult to accept was Jesus's invitation, "Come, follow me." Give up your position in society, your friends and family, your areas of competence and familiarity, and follow me. For it is in this state of vulnerability and abandonment that our essential capacity to "change the world" is revealed.

The truth, which is both destabilizing and empowering, is that all we have are hearts to love and be loved. It is so simple. And yet there may be nothing more difficult.

St. Paul speaks of this in his First Letter to the Corinthians.

> If I speak in the tongues of men and of angels, but have not love, I am a noisy gong or a clanging cymbal. And if I have prophetic powers, and understand all mysteries and all knowledge, and if I have all faith, so as to remove mountains, but have not love, I am nothing If I give away all I have, and if I deliver my body to be burned, but have not love, I will gain nothing. (1 Corinthians 13:1–3)

There is a danger in reading this text in a polarized or binary sense. In emphasizing the primacy of love, we can become cynical of higher education, of government bodies, and of wealth. This is naïve. Knowledge, social structures, and material sustenance are part of reality. Paul does not imply that we ought not to learn languages, pursue scientific knowledge, deepen in our faith practice, or seek to live ideals of charity and sacrifice. His message is subtler and more challenging. Wherever we are in life, whatever our gifts or situation, we can change the world by simply embodying love in what we do. There is a vital—vital in the sense of life-giving—tension between the heart and the head that must be maintained. We can love wisely, not throwing ourselves into an utter admiration of the other but using our knowledge, our skills, and our service as vehicles of love. That changes everything. The rich young man may have given away all of his possessions to the poor, but if he did not "follow Jesus," if he did not seek then to grow in love, it would mean nothing. Love is the source of *life* in what we do.

Many assistants who come to L'Arche are not unlike that student of mine. They want to change the world and they want to develop the skills to do so effectively. They come so that they can learn how to provide a secure and caring environment for people with disabilities, becoming competent in giving showers, in checking medication, even in developing their knowledge of psychology and pedagogy so as to meet the needs of core members. They understand how to be of service in the day-to-day and they are happy to be helpful.

After a time of working this way, an assistant will probably get quite tired and disillusioned. The work is heavy. Days are long, and breaks seem to pass too quickly. She will only be able to last in L'Arche if she discovers how to live each moment with love. The shower is important not just because it is about caring for the body of a core member, but because of the time spent together. Cooking is not just about putting food on the table, but about cutting carrots together, laughing about failed recipes, or preparing a special birthday meal. Time spent together in the evening is not just for the benefit of core members, it is also a chance for everyone to relax, to tell about things that are new in their lives, to enjoy one another's presence.

Like the rich man, we can strip ourselves down to the essence of our humanity. Rich or poor, addict or academic, policy-maker or musician, we all have a capacity to love and to be loved. We all are called to grow in this love, to love more unconditionally, to love more wisely.

Therein lies the answer to how we can be of service to one another and to the world: love. We must grow in our capacity to love one another; we must grow in our openness to receiving love.

CHAPTER ELEVEN

What Is the Nature of Love?

Let us begin by saying that the nature of love is that meeting between the mother and the child. This doesn't seem very spiritual but rather quite physical: a meeting through touch, through the body, through the eyes, through the smile, through the laughter. The child discovers that he or she is loved. And because she is loved, she is someone. Love will always entail the eyes and the physical touch in some way. It is about the glance between the teacher and the pupil who has been disruptive in class. The way the loving teacher looks at the child is not to say, "You are no good." It is to look at him in a friendly way and say, "You can do better. You are a beautiful person. Your behavior merits a consequence so that you understand that it is disruptive to the others and impedes your own education. But fundamentally, you are a beautiful person."

Love implies always speaking to the person behind the behavior, behind the capacity and knowledge. Behind the angers, behind the fear, behind the anguish, there is *you*! Love is not just a way of looking, it is also a way of listening, of being present, of understanding, of helping the other to change and to grow. This means that love implies humility. To love the child who is acting so aggravatingly, or to love the grandparent that always is forgetting my name, demands some effort. To love someone who is not looking and is not paying attention, or to knock on the door of someone we do not really want to see, is a challenge. Love is not about helping people to be the way that we want them to be or the way we think that they should be. It is unconditional. Love implies that we have the desire to help people to be fully themselves.

I would like to tell you about Pauline, a woman that we welcomed into our community in 1970. One of her arms and one of her legs was paralyzed. She was epileptic and diabetic. But what characterized her was her extraordinary violence. She was in a rage, and it is very difficult to live in our little L'Arche homes with someone who is often yelling, screaming, and breaking things. With the help of our psychiatrist, we asked ourselves how we could help Pauline. He reminded us that Pauline had lived forty years of humiliation. She had been looked down upon, mocked, seen as an idiot; her parents were upset, even angry, to have a daughter like that. They probably dreamed of having a daughter who would be admired. They probably hoped to be grandparents someday. Her sisters also looked down upon her, as an embarrassment to the family. At school she was laughed at both because of her physical disability and because of her intellectual disability. In public, people would stare at her. This was the 1940s and 1950s, when people like Pauline were institutionalized and kept hidden from the rest of society. So she was someone who had been terribly humiliated. And when someone has been humiliated, they develop a broken self-image. They come to hate aspects of themselves: an arm that is paralyzed, a brain function that triggers seizures. They begin to hate in themselves that which seems to be the cause of their rejection. They embody division. And division, as we discussed earlier, leads to suffering.

Human suffering, humiliation, can bring any one of us into a depression. I become closed up, I assume that I am no good, I want to hide myself from the rest of the world. It can also bring us to a place of violence. I try to fight my way through life, to fight all these people who reject and scorn me.

The challenge for those of us living with Pauline, our psychiatrist said, was to always see Pauline underneath her violence, underneath her anger, underneath her depression. The challenge was to be present to Pauline the beloved. What does this mean? We come back to the question, what is the nature of love?

St. Paul writes in his First Letter to the Corinthians:

> Love is patient and kind; love is not jealous or boastful; it is
> not arrogant or rude. Love does not insist on its own way; it is
> not irritable or resentful; it does not rejoice at wrong, but finds
> joy in the truth. Love bears all things, trusts all things, hopes
> all things, endures all things. (1 Corinthians 13:4–7)

Love is patient. Patience is when others are so annoying, they make you climb the wall or make you feel like you just cannot stand another minute in their presence. This is how we learn patience. We learn, as we learned with Pauline, to see that the other person has been hurt. We begin to see that humiliation has created divisions and layers, hiding the beloved person within. Patience is waiting. It is about waiting for beauty to be revealed. It is about trusting that you are an integral and unique part of the human family. It is about believing that in you there is something more precious than your apparent anger and anguish. It is about accepting your feelings and waiting for your innermost identity to be revealed. Patience is like waiting for a seed that has been planted in the ground.

In one of Jesus's parables, he describes a field where weeds sprout up beside the wheat. The workers are concerned and ask the householder if they should take out the weeds. The farmer is wise. He knows about patience, he knows about the acceptance and waiting that it implies. He answers, "No; lest in gathering the weeds you root up the wheat along with them. Let both grow together until the harvest; and at the harvest time I will tell the reapers, 'Gather the weeds first and bind them in bundles to be burned, but gather the wheat into my barn'" (Matthew 13:29–30). Patience implies faithfulness. When our belovedness or another's belovedness is hidden, we must wait. Love is patience.

Love is not jealous. Sometimes Pauline would prefer one assistant to another. Sometimes a particular assistant would be especially attached to her. But love must never become fusion. Fusion is two people coming together and not letting one another grow and evolve separately. This can lead to a sort of dependence, this holding on to one another. The danger of fusion is that neither person's inner self can be revealed because each is too much defined by the other. Love is not about holding on, but about waiting for something to be revealed.

Love is not boastful; it is not arrogant or rude. Love does not insist on its own way. Pauline's violence would often compel those around her to try to prove that they were more powerful, that they were stronger, louder, more stubborn. And yet love is about serving. It is about humbly being with the other. I am not here to prove that I am better than you. I am a human person like you are, a child of God like you are. We are each unique. Our stories are different; our gifts are different. But ultimately we are equal in our indispensability to the human family. And to seek our own advantage, to seek to be better than the other, to conquer the other, is to deny our fundamental unity. As St. Paul so eloquently describes, "there are many parts, but one body.... If one member suffers, all suffer together; if one member is honored, all rejoice together" (1 Corinthians 12:20, 26).

Love does not rejoice at wrong, but finds joy in the truth. Love never shirks from honesty, even when it seems difficult. It would have done nothing for Pauline had we pretended that she did not have a disability or if we ignored her violence as if it did not bother everyone else in the household, as if it did not rupture relationships around her. Of course, there is a right and a wrong way of being truthful. To love Pauline was not to put the reality of her disability and of her violence brutally before her. This had been happening all her life! But it was to love her authentically, to grow ourselves so that we could truly be happy to be with her.

Truth is about unity. We can see this in paradoxes where contradicting images or ideas are united because they reveal something true (the term "servant leader," for example). Truth resonates; it is constant. Oneness or unity for Pauline meant coming to know the beauty of her body. So long as she was in rejection of it, she could not be peaceful. It was important for the assistants who helped her with showers and her bath to do so with respect and reverence. It was important for Pauline to have her hair done in a particular way that she wanted, to be helped to buy clothes that made her feel beautiful and perfume that she chose. It was not to reveal the beauty of her body *despite* her disability, but *with* it. It was to help her know the truth that she was beautiful.

This truth was revealed through tenderness. We have talked about the relationship of mother and child, and this is essentially tenderness. At first it is the way to approach a weak person, a fragile person, a vulnerable person. But then we discover that it is not just the approach. It is a way of looking with respect, with welcome, and with admiration at the beauty that is perhaps just barely visible.

Icons of Mary and the baby Jesus embody this love, the tenderness of the mother. But it is much more than this. Mary was also at the foot of the cross (see John 19:25). When Jesus was dying, maybe had even cried out, I can only imagine that her presence was one of incredible tenderness. Jesus had been living humiliation. He was mocked, he was considered a failure for not liberating Israel, he was abandoned by those whom he had called friends. Those who have been humiliated, those who have been hurt and rejected, need a special tenderness. People who have a broken self-image, who are certain that they are no good, need tenderness. They seem to call it forth from within us; for example, the grouchy old man whose eyes become soft and whose hand becomes gentle as he holds his first grandchild.

Tenderness comes forth when we are in the presence of the newborn and when we are in the presence of the dying. Yet, if it is present at the beginning and end of our lives, we can be certain that it is present in the middle as well. Somewhere, we are all little children. And somewhere, we are all in the process of dying. Somewhere, we are all humiliated, we are all wounded, we are all rejected. Tenderness then arises out of our own vulnerability, out of compassion. It is something that we receive so that we may give it, a grace that passes through us. Tenderness is love.

Love is always ready to make allowances...to endure whatever comes. The important thing for Pauline was simply to become a friend. It was to realize that her violence was her way of asking, "Do you love me?" Pauline was inviting us into a relationship with her, just as we were inviting her into a relationship with us, a mutual invitation of friendship that goes beyond serving or assisting. Friendship is the gradual realization that being with the other touches very deep chords. There is a bonding, a sense that the other has brought something special to us. There is a certain humbleness because we have admiration for the other. With Pauline, this presence would be in precious moments. Maybe she would look up and say "Thank you." Maybe our eyes would meet, and that was enough. But all of this took a long time. The moments of presence come between occasions of her broken side coming up—anger, rejection, and jealousy. And so it is a long road. It can take many, many years.

Love is to trust, to hope. Trust comes from a sense of oneness, the sense that we are all in this together. It is the unwavering belief that we are all part of one human family. The pedagogy of L'Arche is to say in all things, "I am happy to live with you." It is our joy in the day-to-day, which reveals that each person is precious and important.

Trust came from our bond with Pauline, a bond of friendship. A sense of unity followed because of our belief in the belovedness within her. And she too could only begin to trust when she was anchored in that secure oneness of friendship. We greeted Pauline with a smile, and we found authentic ways of showing her that we were pleased just to be in her presence. We genuinely desired that she be well, that she be happy, that she know that she was loved. Desire and hope are quite close to one another. But desire becomes hope when we trust that what we long for will come about. We trust that in ways barely perceptible, what we long for is becoming a reality. Trust overcomes the division between what is and what we are moving toward. Trust then alleviates the suffering of desire so that we live in *hope*.

Pauline taught me to love; she taught me to know more intimately the nature of love and to grow in it. To love and to be loved is our greatest capacity and our greatest challenge. "I say this to you, love your enemies and pray for those who persecute you" (Matthew 5:44, NJB).[8] This is the work of peacemaking: patience, kindness, openness, humility, acceptance and respect, forgiveness, truth, trust, hope. As we grow in these, we grow in love. St. Paul continues in his letter to the Corinthians:

> When I was a child, I used to talk like a child, and see things as a child does, and think like a child; but now that I have become an adult, I have finished with all childish ways. Now we see only reflections in the mirror, mere riddles; but then we shall be seeing face to face. Now I can know only imperfectly; but then I shall know just as fully as I am myself known. As it is, these remain: faith, hope and love, the three of them; and the greatest of them is love. (1 Corinthians 13:11–13, NJB)

The nature of love is revealed at the beginning of our lives—the child in her mother's arms. And so to grow in our humanity is to grow to be like a child. There is a beautiful similarity between the very young and the very old, one that we touched upon as we discussed tenderness. To grow in love is to grow toward an encounter with the other, face to face. It is to know the other—to know the one who is weaker and in need as well as the one who is crushing and persecuting—as beloved, just as we know that we are beloved.

We cannot do this on our own. We must discover some strength, must look to some fundamental source of love. And here, I am speaking of course of God. As John reveals in his first letter:

> Beloved, let us love one another; for love is of God and he who loves is born of God and knows God. He who does not love does not know God; for God is love.... No [one] has ever seen God; if we love one another, God abides in us and his love is perfected in us. (1 John 4:7–8, 12)

Remember that earlier we asked ourselves how we know that God exists. As John writes, "No one has ever seen God," but we do know love. We know that love is better than hatred. We know that love is what changes the world. We know that love is something over and above us, something that we must grow in; a "power, working in us, [that] can do infinitely more than we can ask or imagine" (Ephesians 3:20, NJB). Now we see that if we know love, we know God. The nature of love is then the nature of God.

CHAPTER TWELVE

How Does God Intervene in Human Affairs?

Something I feel deeply is that God loves people. God hopes, yearns, desires for people to be happy—that people not get caught up in evil. We can so easily be tempted by our desire to be the best, by wanting to win. You see, deep within us, there is a longing for God, a longing for the infinite. At the very depths of our being is a desire to be loved infinitely. And because we are unsure if we are capable or worthy of receiving such an intimate and unconditional love, we have anguish. This is very important to what it means to be human, and we will come back to it. Our human desire for the infinite can become greed, competition, and individual ambition. We want more money, more recognition, and, we think, more than the next guy. What is a very human longing—the longing to love the one who loves us—becomes twisted and causes us to crush one another. This is certainly not what God wants, for "God so *loved* the world," God so loves each and every one of us, "that he gave his only Son" (John 3:16) to embody this love and become our friend.

This certainty about God's love is deeply ingrained within me. I began L'Arche because I knew that each person in the institution that I visited is important. God so loves everybody! We can see this even in the story of Adam and Eve. God created them with care, gave them a beautiful garden in which to live, and gave them the breath of life so that they would come alive, so that they would be free. But then there was that terrible temptation (which we maybe all have at some moment), when they thought: Wouldn't it be better for us to have all knowledge, all power, and to know all things about human affairs so that we can decide for ourselves what is good or not good for humanity? Somewhere inside of us all, there is a desire to know God, a desire in some ways to *be* God. This was right at the beginning of humanity. We have spoken about this story earlier. But then, even after they seemed to have messed up everything, God came looking for them, calling out, "Where are you?" In the same way, God comes looking for us, full of concern, full of love.

God intervenes in human affairs by calling to each person. Each of us has a conscience drawing us toward truth and justice. God intervenes through every person who is willing to abandon personal gain and ambition in order to give themselves to the bringing together of the world in peace. God's deepest desire is that we become one in love, one with him and one with each other. God intervenes discretely and respectfully, changing one heart and then another, to realize this magnificent vision.

There are many things we do not know about our human history. We tell it and retell it in different ways so as to understand our world today. One version is that the history of humanity is increasingly violent, catastrophic, and out of control. We have developed weapons that can destroy every person on the planet. We are consuming resources on the planet in such a way that ecological systems are being devastated and hundreds of species are dying out. Radical branches of religions and politics seem to be gaining momentum, a development which polarizes conversations and increases the volume of political debate without coming to solutions. This version is the story of war.

It is not untrue. But it is also true that the history of humanity bears witness to God's intervention, guiding us toward a world of peace.

Let us remember that humans began by living in small groupings. Of course they varied enormously depending upon geography and other factors. But there were always these groups. It seems that as a group got larger, some people would leave and form another group. I am not an expert in this field, but I know that there are various ways of tracking the evolution of these communities. One is by looking at language. In Papua New Guinea, for example, there are 734 languages, each belonging to a small village region. The languages are so distinct and significant that people who are from a particular village refer to it as "my Tok"—my talk—rather than the village name. Although the languages have become very diverse, it is thought that they derive from a common stem. Several families of languages have been identified based on similarities in structure and grammar. This indicates a gradual dispersal of the Papua New Guinea population over time. The geography of Papua New Guinea is mountainous, so groups were isolated from one another once they separated. Thus languages were able to evolve quite separately from one another.

In a similar way, in countless groups around the world, traditions and rituals around eating, marriage, relationship to God, politics, art, and music have developed quite uniquely.

There is a story here of division and separation. As we still see today, conflicts arose. These human groupings wanted more land and access to particular resources. They grew in power so as to defend their territory and expand what was theirs. As transportation and food production improved, possibilities increased for contact between what had become an enormous diversity of human beings worldwide. For some, this led to a period of greed-driven conquest, colonization, and war. Leaders, kings, and political heads of state were caught up in a desire for power, obliterating their consciences. Initially their desire may have been for survival, but eventually it became disproportionate and out of control, a desire to accumulate land and riches.

Other developments demonstrate the insuppressible desire for peace that is of God and within each of us. In North America, Mohawk, Onondaga, Oneida, Cayuga, Seneca, and Tuscarora nations joined together in their diversity, creating the Iroquois Confederacy or "Six Nations." This confederacy is united under the "Great Law of Peace," which was revealed by Dekanawidah and Hiawatha.

We can see that in a way, humanity was developing in two directions. One was toward conflicts, wars, and the growth of empires. The other was the coming together of groups in harmony and peacefulness. Even the establishment of intentional peace evolved into a gradual recognition of the horrors of war and evil.

Coming from a more European perspective, I can see a peak or a double climax after the Second World War. In particular, the world was faced with two horrific realities. One was Auschwitz, the most notorious of Hitler's concentration camp networks. Over one million people were murdered there. Nine out of ten of these people were Jewish. Others included Polish resisters, the Romani people, Soviet prisoners of war, homosexual men and women, and people with intellectual disabilities. The word *holocaust* means "wholly burned." Thus it is a fitting description of the unfathomable genocide that took place in Europe in the early twentieth century.

The other peak is the American detonation of the atomic bomb in Japan, first on Hiroshima on August 6, 1945, and then on Nagasaki on August 9, 1945. Over one hundred thousand people were killed directly, and tens of thousands more were affected by the radiation. This is the only time in history that nuclear weapons have been deployed for warfare, and the ethics of their use is still highly contested. It seems to me that any destruction of life on this scale can never be justified. But that is just my opinion.

In these distinct events, we see the turning away from God or a perversion of the desire for proximity to the infinite God. We began to discuss this a little bit at the beginning of the chapter. And here we see the disastrous outcomes when our longing to know God is not recognized as such and is not lived with humility and wonderment. Too quickly, it can become a desire to *be* God.

Hitler's vision was one of purity, a pure race, which presumably implied harmony and peace. He did not see the purity that already exists in our amazing diversity—the purity of the human family. We are each unique parts of one human body; we are each precious and beloved. Hitler's perverse ideology necessitated a powerful and bloody imposition, as well as dictatorship. This is utterly against God who works in ways beyond our imagining and who calls us to participate, not with power and control, but with abandonment and trust.

Atomic research is about a desire to know the infinite, a desire to know the source of all things. Albert Einstein, one of the most significant and influential scientists of the twentieth century, was a pacifist and a man with great respect for nature and curiosity about the world. Curiosity motivated his research, but he was at the mercy of politicians with a compulsive need to dominate. Even science, which begins in a spirit of wonderment, may bear the fruit of destruction. Again, God invites us to learn, to explore, to know God through our experiences, through science and this amazing creation, but always with reverence and humility. When we begin to seek our own advantage, we crush life.

In 1948, the Universal Declaration of Human Rights was adopted by the United Nations General Assembly. The first two articles are beautiful. They seem to be rooted in the horrific events of the first half of the century, not unlike flowers growing out of compost:

> All human beings are born free and equal in dignity and rights. They are endowed with reason and conscience and should act towards one another in a spirit of brotherhood.
>
> Everyone is entitled to all the rights and freedoms set forth in this Declaration, without distinction of any kind, such as race, colour, sex, language, religion, political or other opinion, national or social origin, property, birth or other status. Furthermore, no distinction shall be made on the basis of the political, jurisdictional or international status of the country or territory to which a person belongs, whether it be independent, trust, non-self-governing or under any other limitation of sovereignty.[9]

What emerged here was the articulation of a subtle unity in our human family. It is not the *re*articulation of our oneness, because it comes with a growing sense of appreciation for the diversity and uniqueness of each human being. Jewish people are amazing and beautiful people! It is an outrage that they have been persecuted when each individual is precious. It became clear that a Jewish man or woman should not be identified simply as being Jewish. Nor should a Christian be defined by her Christianity. Nor a German or an American by his nationality. The emerging sense of oneness is about the dignity of each unique human being, a dignity which unites us in our difference.

So we can see this beautiful movement of humanity. In one way, it is a dissection of our social identities, the peeling away of labels that define us too narrowly—Christian, Muslim, American, Mexican, gay, straight, liberal, conservative. But at the same time, it is the realization of a universal togetherness. This paradox of unity in diversity is humanity's story of peace. It is a movement toward human fulfillment, which is to fulfill the desire for peace not war, for love and not hate. There is something deep inside this movement toward the unity of reality.

How does God intervene in the long evolution from closed up groups with separate traditions and languages to opened up groups—groups that recognize the beauty and value of every person in each group? In this long evolution and movement of humanity, God intervenes discretely by inviting individual men and women to become men and women of peace, participating in the realization of God's vision of unity. God draws each person through his or her personal conscience toward justice, truth, and love.

God is always inviting us to grow in love because God loves us and cannot bear to see us suffer or inflict suffering upon one another. Throughout history, women and men have risen up and made God's invitation more visible, more audible. We discuss several in this book, including Dekanawidah, Dorothy Day, Aung San Suu Kyi, Mohandas (Mahatma) Gandhi, Martin Luther King, Jr., Etty Hillesum, Malala Yousafzai, Abdul Ghaffar Khan, Sophie and Hans Scholl, Dietrich Bonhoeffer, Dorothy Day, Tony Walsh, and Vandana Shiva.

Others are lesser known. Recently, I was reading about a group called the "Richmond 16," sixteen men from Richmond, England, who refused to join the British military in 1916. The Military Service Act of 1916 had introduced conscription for all men between ages eighteen and forty-one, but those with religious or political objections could appeal to a (rather skeptical) tribunal. Some were granted a non-combatant or nonmilitary role. The Richmond 16 refused to participate in the war effort in any way. Although they were diverse in their denominational and political affiliations—Quaker, Methodist, Jehovah's Witness, Socialist, Congregationalist, and Anglican—they were united in their conviction that war was utterly un-Christian and inhumane. They wrote on the walls of the prison where they were detained, "Thou shall not kill," and "You might as well try to dry a floor by throwing water on it as to try and end this war by fighting." The men were taken to a miserable dungeon in France where they were tortured, became ill with dysentery, and were threatened with death. Eventually, they were released, but their reintegration into a war-friendly society was not easy.[10]

Today we have a special name for people who are willing to go against the mainstream because of what they know to be true. We call men and women who are unwilling to act against their conscience "conscientious objectors." Since the beginning of human recollection, stories have been recounted of women and men who rise up and give a direction of humanity, inviting us to follow the way of peace. They are men and women who seem to have a particular openness to God, however that is articulated.

We also can look to the first books of the Bible to explore how God intervenes in the world. God sends forth prophets, strong men and women, who proclaim God's love and who call out people in society and culture for straying from the way of peace. Through words and actions, these prophets bring people to freedom.

There is Moses, to whom God says:

> "I have indeed seen the misery of my people in Egypt. I have heard them crying for help on account of their taskmasters. Yes, I am well aware of their sufferings. And I have come down to rescue them from the clutches of Egyptians and bring them up out of that country, to a country rich and broad, to a country flowing with milk and honey…I am sending you to Pharaoh, for you to bring my people the Israelites out of Egypt." Moses said to God, "Who am I to go to Pharaoh and bring the Israelites out of Egypt?" "I shall be with you," God said. (Exodus 3:7–8; 10–21, NJB)

It is amazingly tender: "I have indeed seen the misery of my people." God so loves the world!

Moses demonstrates not only the strength and daring of prophets of peace, but what is most important: humility and trust. "Who am I to go to Pharaoh?" he asks. Surely there is someone more suited to the job, someone who knows more, who is stronger and more charismatic. God responds, "I shall be with you." And Moses trusts in God.

To Jeremiah, God reveals a beautiful vision of conscience: "Before I formed you in the womb I knew you; before you came to birth I consecrated you; I appointed you as prophet to the nations." (Jeremiah 1:5, NJB)

Humility and trust are quite similar to abandonment and trust, which we discussed earlier when we spoke about conscience. Humility is like abandonment because it is about letting go of one's self—one's ego, one's personal projects and one's ambitions—for something bigger, something beyond individual control or scope. John the Baptist describes it perfectly when he says, "It is the bridegroom who has the bride; and yet the bridegroom's friend, who stands there and listens to him, is filled with joy at the bridegroom's voice. This is the joy I feel and it is complete. He must grow greater and I must grow less" (John 3:29–30, NJB). Humility is living with abandonment to the movement of life, the movement of peace.

God's interventions become integrated into society through traditions. Religious practices are structures given to us so that we may be taught to listen to our conscience, so that together we may be guided into a personal relationship with God. But God's interventions cannot be constrained. Even after the Jewish people are freed from Egyptian rule, God continues to send prophets who denounce their lack of listening and who invite the people to greater openness, to greater listening, to greater truth and love.

Through Amos, God says: "I hate, I despise your feasts, and I take no delight in your solemn assemblies...let justice roll down like waters, and righteousness like an everflowing stream." (Amos 5:21, 24)

Through Isaiah, we see God angered by ostentatious fasting, by our seeking to impress others and show off our goodness or piety:

> Is not this the fast that I choose: to loose the bonds of wickedness, to undo the thongs of the yoke, to let the oppressed go free, and to break every yoke? Is it not to share your bread with the hungry, and bring the homeless poor into your house; when you see the naked, to cover him, and not to hide yourself from your own flesh? (Isaiah 58:6–7)

The prophet Isaiah reveals in many ways God's beautiful vision for humanity:

"On this mountain, the Lord of hosts will make for all peoples a feast of fat things, a feast of wine on the lees, of fat things full of marrow, of wine on the lees well refined. And [God] will destroy on this mountain the covering that is cast over all peoples, the veil that is spread over all nations. [God] will swallow up death for ever, and the Lord God will wipe away tears from all the faces, and the reproach of [God's] people [God] will take away from the earth; for the Lord has spoken." (Isaiah 25:6–8)

God's invitation is for *all people* to come to a "feast of fat things," to be part of this unity in friendship: "They shall beat their swords into plowshares, and their spears into pruning hooks; nation shall not lift up sword against nation, neither shall they learn war any more." (Isaiah 2:4)

And then, Isaiah reveals the greatest of all the prophets, the Messiah: "For to us a child is born, to us a son is given...and his name will be called, 'Wonderful Counselor, Mighty God, Everlasting Father, Prince of Peace.'" (Isaiah 9:6)

God sent the greatest of all prophets, the Messiah that the Jewish people were waiting for: Jesus, the beloved son of the Father. Jesus is the Word made flesh, the *embodiment* of God's love and longing for communion in love. Communion is God, which is the fulfillment of humanity. This deepest desire is revealed throughout humanity and it is expressed eloquently in Jesus's prayer the night before his crucifixion:

> That they may all be one;
> even as thou, Father, art in me,
> and I in thee,
> that they also may be in us,
> so that the world may believe that thou hast sent me.

The glory which thou hast given me I have given to them,
that they may be one even as we are one,
I in them and thou in me,
that they may become perfectly one,
so that the world may know that thou hast sent me
and hast loved them even as thou hast loved me.
...
I made known to them thy name,
and I will make it known,
that the love with which thou hast loved me may be in them,
and I in them.
(John 17:21–23, 26)

Jesus does not want the earthly or temporal power of a ruling king. Rather, he wants to become the king of our hearts. He wants us to follow him on the road to love. This is the desire that motivates the movement of peace and unity we have been discovering, confirmed by eruptions of God, of the Word of God, into humanity. God enters our world through prophets of peace who listen to their conscience: conscientious objectors and men and women who speak out about injustice and who dare to speak the truth even when everyone else remains silent, who share God's passionate desire for the human family to come together in love.

God sent Jesus into the world—the incarnation of love, truth, justice, and peace—so that we can *know* these values intimately. Jesus promises his friends, his disciples, that he will send the Holy Spirit, the Paraclete, to teach us and help us all to become prophets and messengers of peace.

God does not always intervene in big ways, but in little ways by the willingness of human beings to grow in the wisdom and the love of

God. Some prophets of peace have been well known. But many are not. Still, they are sources of joy, love, and life in their communities, living with abandonment and trust, bringing people together. God is in all of those who stand just outside of our structures of law and religion, of cultural norms and expectations. God is in those who dare to escape these walls and barriers and who call us to do the same: who call us individually and as a society to discover our fundamental unity in belovedness.

God wants each one of us, wherever we are, to intervene in the evolution of our world. This can be through acts of love that break down barriers of fear in others. It is part of my own prayer: I ask God to eliminate in others and in me any seed of hatred that keeps us apart from one another. This work of peace happens within us, but we need God's help. There is a wonderful mutuality. We need God to dwell within us, guiding us toward truth and love. And God longs for us, longs for us to turn to God and dwell in God's love.

CHAPTER THIRTEEN

If God Is Good and All-Powerful,
How Can Evil Exist?

L et us begin by looking at the first part of this question. "If God is good and all-powerful..." What does that mean? Perhaps we must look again at the nature of God, the nature of God's intervention and of his relationship with us. There is a beautiful text in Revelation where Jesus says, "Behold, I stand at the door and knock; if anyone hears my voice and opens the door, I will come in to him and eat with him, and him with me" (Revelation 3:20).

Here is the simplicity of God's intervention and invitation to us: Jesus stands at the door and knocks. Maybe I don't want him to come in. Maybe I am too caught up in the motor of activity, and so I don't hear him knocking. And if I *do* hear him, I just don't have time to stop.

What we hear in this passage is the deep and loving respect of God, knocking at the door of our hearts, hoping to come in to live in us and to teach us how to love. "I give you a new commandment: love one another; you must love one another just as I have loved you" (John 13:34, NJB). We can only love if we are willing to open the door of our hearts and allow Jesus to dwell in us. This is part of Jesus's prayer the night before he was betrayed: "With me in them and you in me, may they be so perfected in unity that the world will recognize that it was you who sent me and that you have loved them as you have loved me" (John 17:23, NJB). Are we willing to open the door?

We are beginning to understand the incredible respect of God for our freedom. God does not break down the doors of our hearts. Our freedom is such that we may, for example, become part of the Mafia, like that man I told you about in chapter 8. He was abused, so he believed he had to be strong to protect himself from future abuse. Somehow he was not able to open the door to God; he wanted to be powerful on his own! He didn't want to be weak. The extraordinary thing is that God is standing at the door and waiting.

I appreciate these words of Etty Hillesum, written in the heat of the Holocaust:

> Dear God, these are anxious times. Tonight for the first time I lay in the dark with burning eyes as scene after scene of human suffering passed before me.... But one thing is becoming increasingly clear to me: that You cannot help us, that we must help You to help ourselves. And that is all we can manage these days and also all that really matters: that we safeguard that little piece of You, God, in ourselves. And perhaps in others as well.[11]

Remember the question at the beginning of the Gospel of John, "Where are you staying" (John 1:38)? That is the question we all have. Where does God dwell? Here Hillesum says that God dwells within us, but that we must make room, we must "safeguard" this God whose presence within brings us peace in the midst of suffering and hardship, whose presence helps us to love our enemies and to be free of fear and hatred. Hillesum also writes, "I am nevertheless grateful for that kosher

German soldier at the kiosk with his bag of carrots and cauliflowers [who was kind to me]...I shall have to pray for this German soldier. Out of all the uniforms one has been given a face now."[12]

God is constantly inviting us to "come and see," but we must always be opening the door. We must open our ears to the word of God, our eyes to the wonders of creation, and our hearts to the pain and the beauty of our brothers and sisters.

Have you ever waited outside someone's door, knocking? You know that the person is home, but you have the feeling that she doesn't want to see you. If you are just delivering a parcel and don't really care about her, you might be angry because you want to be on your way and finish your route, so it's not a really big problem. You will have forgotten all about it by the end of the day. But if you really *love* the person you are waiting for and you desperately want to see her because she is precious to you, waiting can be really painful. What is she doing in there? Did she forget that I was coming? Doesn't she want to see me? This is painful.

We discover in this example our wounded God; a God that has been hurt; a God that we are rejecting and humiliating. We discover, dare I say, the tears of God.

Jesus was humiliated on the cross:

> The passers-by jeered at him; they shook their heads and said, "So you would destroy the Temple and in three days rebuild it! Then save yourself, if you are God's son and come down from the cross!" The chief priests with the scribes and elders mocked him in the same way, with the words, "He saved others; he cannot save himself. He is the king of Israel, let him come down from there and we will believe in him. He has put his trust in God; now let God rescue him if he wants him.

For he did say, 'I am God's son.'" Even the bandits who were crucified with him taunted him in the same way. (Matthew 27:39–44, NJB)

Jesus was abandoned, condemned, and ridiculed by his own people and by the leaders of his religion. In the same way that some of Jesus's friends may have expected him to "come down from the cross," some of us may have an expectation that our all-powerful God does not need to knock but can push the door right down! Even his disciples had this hope. But God doesn't do that: Jesus is crucified. The cross reveals to us this mystery of the weakness and vulnerability of love.

Some people have a hard time accepting the vulnerability of God. Once I received a letter to that effect, someone who was outraged and offended that I would suggest Jesus could be humiliated and wounded, that Jesus was not a tower of strength. Many people have a vision of God the almighty conqueror who, even when he died, was a strong person, defiant upon the cross. They do not want to accept that Jesus was in pain, abandoned, that he cried out to God, "'Eli, Eli, lama sabachthani?' that is, 'My God, my God, why have you forsaken me?'" (Matthew 27:46, NJB) This revelation can be almost threatening for people who need a strong God, a powerful savior.

Some of the disciples felt similarly. You can imagine their anticipation as Jesus came into Jerusalem to great shouts of Hosanna. Here at last was a leader who could free the people from the oppression of the Roman occupation! He had raised Lazarus from the dead, so the disciples already knew that he was capable of great things.

The next day a great crowd who had come to the feast heard that Jesus was coming to Jerusalem. So they took branches of palm trees and went out to meet him, crying, "Hosanna! Blessed is he who comes in the name of the Lord, even the King of Israel!" And Jesus found a young ass and sat upon it; as it is written, "Fear not, daughter of Zion; behold, your king is coming, sitting on an ass's colt!" His disciples did not understand this at first; but when Jesus was glorified, then they remembered that this had been written of him and had been done to him. The crowd that had been with him when he called Lazarus out of the tomb and raised him from the dead bore witness. (John 12:12–17)

Jesus rides in upon a donkey and not a horse. A donkey was an animal of peace, a horse was an animal of war. Wasn't Jesus coming to overthrow the occupation? I am touched by the admission that at first, "his disciples did not understand this." Perhaps they, like the person who sent me a letter, would have said something a bit angry had someone pointed out to them the paradox of his entrance. They were not yet ready to accept the littleness and fragility of Jesus.

Maurice Zundel, a Swiss priest and theologian, wrote beautifully and insightfully about this unexpected nature of God. In a similar way to Etty Hillesum, he wrote that we "must reverse all our perspectives: it is not us, it is God that must be saved. God must be saved from ourselves, just as music must be saved from our noise, truth from our fantasies, and love from our possession."[13]

How often in history has God been invoked to justify conquest, to justify seizing power, to justify oppression or the subjugation of a group of people under some tyranny? There are many examples: from the Crusades to North American residential schools to radical Zionists to militant jihadists. How easily we can wound God, who desires our unity and whose deepest desire is that *all* people be gathered together. We must save God from our own compulsive need for power.

Zundel writes, "Fragile God...the most astonishing revelation of the Gospel: a fragile God is placed in our hands, a fragile God is entrusted to our conscience.... This is the light of the Cross: God dies for Love of those who refuse obstinately to love Him."[14]

Since God is love, we might also read that God is wounded when we refuse to love. It is that simple.

We have spoken before of conscience—that little voice calling us into the way of peace, the attraction to truth and love, to justice and to freedom. It is born when we have a sense of *I am*, when we have a sense of the presence of God within us. We have seen how easy it is for conscience to be stifled, so fragile is the presence of God within us. Zundel writes, "There is a universal *I*, a universal *I* hidden in the depths of every human soul, an *I* who gathers us together...fragile, secret, silent like the flame of a candle, and that is the true God. There is no other."[15] God is a vulnerable flame, a little voice, a humble Jesus who is knocking.

People who need a strong God and don't want to accept the vulnerability of Jesus may not be ready to accept that it is not their strength that will lead them into unity in love, but their own vulnerability. Their vision of Christianity is that we must be *strong* and we must announce God *strongly*. They escape the reality of their own weakness by clinging to an almighty and perfect God.

To assert that God is perfect is to say that there's nothing lacking in him. This is a metaphysical theology standpoint. And if there is nothing lacking in him, there can be no suffering and no pain. But if we have come to the simple understanding that "God is love" (1 John 4:8), we might ask ourselves, what is the particular suffering of love? What is the particular suffering of a God who is love?

John also writes that "he who loves is born of God and knows God" (1 John 4:7), and so we can trust that our own experiences of love might reveal to us something of the nature of God and the nature of God's suffering. In Isaiah, God is revealed by an analogy of the love of a mother for her child: "As one whom his mother comforts, so I will comfort you" (Isaiah 66:13). A mother suffers in her love. She is deeply bonded to her child. At one time, they were one body. Then she held him in her arms, and he nursed at her breast. As he grows, she is in wonder. She wants to protect him, to ensure his happiness. At the same time, she hopes that he will become free and grow to be fully himself, which means that he must grow away from her. This can be very painful. When he does not seem to recognize that she is the one who gave him life, she can be deeply wounded. When he is hurt or humiliated, she is torn with compassion and a deep longing to hold him closely again and to soothe his anguish.

This analogy of God the mother is revealing. An analogy is a descriptive mechanism that transfers characteristics from one subject so as to reveal something about another. But an analogy can never fully reveal the subject it is used to describe. While we can learn a lot about God by using this analogy of the mother, it is not quite the same. Notably, a mother is loving whereas God is not a person who loves—God *is love*. We must always be aware that we are moving about the periphery of a great mystery. We can enter into the mystery of God's suffering, we can wrestle with God and question God, but the truth surpasses us in every way.

And yet, as John writes, we may know God even when we do not fully understand God. This is not astounding. We know our friends, but we do not know everything about them. In a similar way, we can know God without knowing everything about God. We can know of God's suffering because somewhere it is closely bonded with our own suffering, the suffering of our belovedness, our anguish.

Anguish helps us to see that we need Jesus, not as a strong force to pull us out of the jaws of temptation, but as an intimate friend to console us. To console means to help that person discover that she is beloved, "You are precious in my eyes" (Isaiah 43:4). To console is to say, "I am with you." Jesus, "became flesh, he lived among us" (John 1:14, NJB) so that he could be fully with us. He came to be with us in our anguish, and he came that we might be with him in his anguish, that we might come to know the suffering of God and to be drawn to God through it. The Word *lived among us* to share our experiences of joy and sorrow, of wonderment and rejection. And the Word *became flesh*, a physical presence of tenderness, so that we would know God's love for each person, so that we would learn to love God.

Sometimes we can be uncertain about the significance of Jesus's body, about the significance of our own bodies. Our bodies are how we live in reality, how we have experiences. We *hear* with our ears, and we *see and watch* with our eyes, and we *touch* with our own hands (see 1 John 1:1, NJB). If the Word became flesh, it was in order to share in our experience of being human.

Our bodies are our instruments of relationship. We need our ears to listen to one another, our eyes to look with tenderness, our hands to hold and to touch with love and respect. It was through touch, through soothing and healing the Mafia man's body, that my friend the doctor became friends with him. It was by coffee and conversation, our eyes meeting, that I became friends with the beggar at Lourdes. The Word became flesh to be fully in relationship with us.

A few days after riding into Jerusalem, Jesus and his disciples gather for the Passover meal. Again, we can imagine their anticipation. Jesus has come into the city (almost) like a hero. Passover is the celebration of the liberation of the Jewish people from slavery in Egypt. It is the perfect occasion for a liberator to take action.

> Jesus, knowing that the Father had given all things into his hands, and that he had come from God and was going to God, rose from supper, laid aside his garments, and girded himself with a towel. Then he poured water into a basin, and began to wash the disciples' feet, and to wipe them with the towel with which he was girded. (John 13:3–5)

It is an astounding act of love and powerlessness. What about mobilizing the multitude to challenge Rome, to challenge the oppression? What about a Messiah who will lead the Jewish people to victory? For the disciples, this is almost a crisis moment. Peter is the first who speaks his discomfort:

> "Lord, do you wash my feet?" Jesus answered him, "What I am doing you do not know now, but afterward you will understand." Peter said to him, "You shall never wash my feet." Jesus answered him, 'If I do not wash you, you have no part in me." Simon Peter said to him, "Lord, not my feet only but also my hands and my head!" Jesus said to him, "He who has bathed does not need to wash, except for his feet, but he is clean all over; and you are clean...." When he had washed their feet, and taken his garments, and resumed his place, he said to them, "Do you know what I have done to you? You call me Teacher and Lord; and you are right, for so I am. If I then,

your Lord and Teacher, have washed your feet, you also ought to wash one another's feet. For I have given you an example, that you also should do as I have done to you. Truly, truly, I say to you, a servant is not greater than his master; nor is he who is sent greater than he who sent him. If you know these things, blessed are you if you do them." (John 13:6–10; 12–17)

He is inviting his disciples into a relationship of mutuality. The master has bent down and washed the feet of his followers and yet, "a servant is not greater than his master." It is not a reversal of hierarchy: it is the abolishment of it. Jesus doesn't want to appear as the all-powerful, for power leaves no space for friendship. Jesus wants to become our friends, if we are willing to have our feet washed, if we are willing to accept him.

True friendship is vulnerable. After putting his robe back on, Jesus speaks a line from Psalm 41. "He who ate my bread has lifted his heel against me." (John 13:18; see also Psalm 41:9)

He is speaking about Judas. Jesus called Judas to become his disciple, to be in a relationship with him, to share bread with him. Yet Judas could not stand Jesus's vulnerability. In the Gospel of John, Judas is mentioned three times. The first time is in the sixth chapter when Jesus offers his flesh and blood as nourishment for those who follow and trust in him. He is offering himself entirely to others so that he may dwell in them as a source of life. Many of his followers find this difficult to accept, including Judas, at which point Jesus refers to him as a devil. The second time that Judas is mentioned is when Mary anoints Jesus's feet with costly perfume in chapter 12. Judas is shocked by the act of love and tenderness, an act that suggests Jesus's mortality and need for comfort. The third time that Judas is mentioned is here in chapter 13: as Jesus washes the feet of the disciples, Judas's growing discomfort with Jesus who is not all-powerful becomes too much to bear.

Sometimes it is easy to imagine that Judas was predetermined as the betrayer of Jesus, a pawn in a great master plan. I think that Judas was someone who was terribly wounded, who was drawn to Jesus because he needed a strong person to follow. And Jesus longed to change his heart, to liberate him from his fears of weakness and vulnerability. Judas was someone terribly fragile. But Jesus's vulnerability was too threatening to Judas, and so when Jesus offers himself to Judas, dipping a morsel of bread and offering it to him in a gesture of friendship, "Satan entered into [Judas]" (John 13:27) Judas becomes overwhelmed by his own anguish, he is enveloped in a terrible fear and hatred, and he leaves to deliver Jesus to the authorities and ultimately to death.

Have you ever been so afraid that you no longer quite have control over your actions? It could be as insignificant-seeming as saying something hurtful about a friend because one doesn't want to appear uncool. It could seem benign—cutting off someone in conversation because something they said brings up anger. It could be misguided—experimenting with sexuality because it seems to affirm one's beauty and value. When we feel anguish, when we have a sense that we do not know who we are, a sense of being profoundly lonely, we become afraid. We can be willing to give up a lot—friendships, communication, even intimacy—so as to protect ourselves from the feeling of being "nobody," the suffering of loneliness, our anguish. It is only when we can see this in ourselves that we can discover freedom from our compulsions. It is only when we begin to recognize the cry of our own hearts that we can respond to the cry of God to be in relationship with us.

God knocks at the door. God longs to share a table with us. God dares to share bread with us, to be that open and that vulnerable. The Gospel passage goes on:

> When Jesus had thus spoken, he was troubled in spirit, and testified, "Truly, truly, I say to you, one of you will betray me." The disciples looked at one another, uncertain of whom he spoke. One of his disciples, whom Jesus loved, was lying close to the breast of Jesus. (John 13:21–23)

Bonds of friendship allow us to sense when someone is anguished, when they need consolation. I think that the disciple whom Jesus loved felt his pain and shared in it. He laid his head against Jesus's breast and could hear Jesus's throbbing and anguished heart. It is Peter who urges John to ask *who* will betray Jesus. John's first instinct is simply to put his head against Jesus's body so as to console him. We can feel God's pain when we bear witness to cruelty and injustice, when we meet people who have turned their backs on love. Rather than pointing fingers, Jesus calls us to lay our heads on his breast. Rather than seeking to crush those who are imprisoned in hatred and fear, we must ourselves grow in love so as to welcome them and help them to grow in relationship.

We have already spoken quite a lot about the latter part of the question, "How can evil exist?" Perhaps we can now add that evil is the rejection of a God of love or, simpler still, the rejection of love and justice. We reject love and justice and the truth of our common humanity because somewhere we are afraid to live a life so vulnerable.

I need help to love. There can be times when I just want to get rid of people who are knocking at the door because they are a pain in the neck. Throughout this little book, we have been discovering the extent to which we protect ourselves, the extent to which we put up barricades of fear and hatred around ourselves to hide our vulnerability. In doing this, we imprison the secret of our humanity—which is that we can find wholeness only through friendship, through fulfillment in relationship, which is friendship with God.

We are coming to the mystery that John reveals in his first letter.

> In this the love of God was made manifest among us, that
> God sent his only Son into the world, so that we might live
> through him.... Beloved, if God so loved us, we also ought to
> love one another...if we love one another, God abides in us
> and his love is perfected in us. (1 John 4:9, 11, 12)

God is perfect and God is love, and still God's love comes to perfection in us. We might come back to the words of the prophet Isaiah: "As a mother comforts a child, so shall I comfort you," God said through the prophet Isaiah (Isaiah 66:13, NJB). A mother is in awe of her child. Her deepest desire is not to make her child obey, but that her child will grow and become freely himself. She does not want to impose that her child ought to love her, but longs deeply for her child to do so freely. This love is vulnerable, open to rejection and to humiliation.

> There is no fear in love, but perfect love casts out fear. For fear
> has to do with punishment, and he who fears is not perfected
> in love. We love, because he first loved us. (1 John 4:18–19)

Perfect love implies that there is no room for fear, for hatred, for evil. Our lives are then a journey of growth, of facing our fears, of opening our hearts to God. God is knocking at our door so that in the oneness of friendship we may welcome this perfect and fearlessly vulnerable love that is God.

CHAPTER FOURTEEN

Is Death the End of Everything?

Shouldn't we begin by saying that life is change? We begin life in the womb of our mother, quickly changing, growing from a few cells, developing a nose, eyes, fingers, toes. And then there is that dramatic and agonizing change which is birth. With this change comes the discovery of a world so much bigger than where we were, a world where the horizons are infinite and we no longer have a sense of our place within them. We have lost that place of security. This is a huge change, a huge loss, and we experience anguish. Anguish, recall, is an existential suffering. It is the suffering of the finite in a reality that is infinite, the suffering of the baby who is limited by skin, by the capacity of her senses in taking in the unlimited world around her. Who am I in all of this?

Every time there is change, there is loss to something. When we move from milk to solid food, we lose a special intimacy with our mother. When we move toward adulthood, we lose some of the freedom of childhood. When we move from adulthood into old age, we lose energy, we lose physical strength, we lose even our hearing, our glasses and so on. In many ways, the movement of life is a movement of loss. Even the cells in our body are continually dying!

Etty Hillesum, writes:

I have come to terms with life…

By "coming to terms with life" I mean: the reality of death has become a definite part of my life; my life has, so to speak, been extended by death, by my looking death in the eye and accepting it, by accepting destruction as part of life and no longer wasting my energies on fear of death or the refusal to acknowledge its inevitability. It sounds paradoxical: by excluding death from our life, we cannot live a full life, and by admitting death into our life, we can enlarge it and enrich it."[16]

Very quickly, we sacrifice a little bit of life because we are afraid of death. We are afraid of anguish, for in death, we do not know what will become of us. If reality is divided, life and death represent the ultimate division. Here she speaks about death, but we can see that the same goes for all loss; we lose a job, we lose a spot in the theater production, we lose a parent or a grandparent, we lose a friendship. The same goes for all change; changing schools, leaving home, entering into a relationship, becoming single. It is about crossing a threshold between then and now, between with and without, between known and unknown, between finite and infinite. It is about overcoming dividedness. And so there is grief, which is a form of anguish.

We can begin to *live* only if, as Hillesum says, "the reality of death has become a definite part of…life." Death is not only a reality of life, it is *integral*; "destruction is a part of life." Every loss leads to growth. But we can dare to look at death, we can only dare to look at our fears and *welcome* that which makes us afraid, only if we have observed that this continual movement of life includes a movement of death.

I would say that one of our greatest fears is humiliation. Humiliation is a rejection by the ambient group, our family and friends, those who are close to us and give us a sense of who we are. Humiliation is a profound loneliness. Nobody wants me, nobody loves me. Whenever we undergo change, we risk humiliation. As we are, we may be accepted by a certain group of people. But if we change, will that still be the case?

It is the anguish of the little child that is loved by her mother. As she grows, as she becomes older, as she begins to do things independently, she wonders: Will she still be loved?

This fear of change, which is really a fear of the anguish that change brings up, is profound and widespread. For example, the Catholic Church has been slow in accepting ecumenism, slow in accepting that we can learn from and share experiences with other churches. The same goes for other religions. If we begin to open up dialogues with other traditions, what do we risk losing about our own identity? Perhaps we will lose something, but in loss there is an opening up to newness and deepening in truth. There is a deepening in faith; there is always a gain.

From that which is rejected, life springs. I once lived in Törbel, Switzerland, at an altitude of nearly seven thousand feet. I remember the farmers going out onto the slopes when the snow was gone. They wore great packs of cow manure and they would spread it on the ground, like butter on toast. They did it with such delicacy and respect, confident in the new life that would spring up from this waste. This is the wonder of compost. In the movement of life, even death is not wasted. The scraps and peelings, the rotten fruits, the moldy bread, the parts of our food that in digestion have nothing more to offer our bodies in terms of energy or vitamins, the utter waste, gives life. Nothing is wasted. All our mistakes, all those things we have done, experiences had that seemed to bring death, that brought loss, in the end have helped me to grow. Because life is not just about taking the "right path"—it is about growth. St. John of the Cross says it is in losing our way that we will discover that this *is* the right way.

The mystery of compost should give us confidence to live experiences, to accept change, to risk loss and to be open to the movement of life. Today we have toilets. We send our garbage far away in great trucks. When we do something that is clearly wrong, we want to send it away, to never see it, to forget about it. But the reality is that our growth comes from those experiences. We make mistakes, and we learn from them. We hurt others and we experience the wonderful gift of forgiveness, which can bring us into a deeper bonding with one another. When we have made a mistake, when we are living in a way that is not about growth, that is not about new life, we must have the confidence to leave this path. Then we must sort the rotten vegetables from the good and cut away the weeds, celebrating that the compost will bring nutrients to the new plants. Compost is integral to growth. Death is integral to life.

Jesus says something similar when he tells us about the grain of wheat that falls into the ground.

> Now the hour has come for the Son of man to be glorified. In all truth I tell you, unless a wheat grain falls into the earth and dies, it remains only a single grain; but if it dies, it yields a rich harvest. Anyone who loves his life loses it; anyone who hates his life in this world will keep it for eternal life. Whoever serves me, must follow me, and my servant will be with me wherever I am. If anyone serves me, the Father will honor him. Now my soul is troubled. What shall I say: Father, save me from this hour? But it is for that very reason that I have come to this hour. Father, glorify your name! (John 12:23–28, NJB)

There is something beautiful and mysterious about a single grain. It is so small, more fragile that a little stone, and just as inconspicuous. And yet there is so much life within it! But for that life to come forth, it must fall from its place among the other grains, fall from a great height, fall away from the sun into the cool and moist earth. There it will begin to disintegrate. But ever so delicately, ever so persistently, a shoot will grow, casting away the remains of what the grain once was, pushing through soil toward the warm promise of sunlight. And from this grain that has died, from this small shoot that is changing and growing, will come a rich harvest.

After giving us this image, Jesus makes clear its relevance for our own lives. "Anyone who loves his life loses it; anyone who hates his life in this world will keep it for eternal life." Although this translation uses the word *life*, there are two different words here in the original Greek: *psuche* and *zoe*. *Psuche* can be described as the animating soul, the energy which activates us in the world. I sometimes translate this directly as our compulsions. Compulsions, recall, are the behaviors that come to fill a void somewhere, that keep us busy without actually accomplishing much. Compulsions are like filling up one's belly with a bag of chips. We are *full* but still hungry. *Psuche* is about living without growing toward fulfillment. *Zoe* is growing to the fullness of life. It is life in its plenitude, life eternal. So perhaps we can rewrite this complicated sounding sentence and see that it is actually quite simple. "Anyone who loves his *psuche* loses it; anyone who hates his *psuche* keeps it for *zoe*."

If we love *psuche*, if we are unwilling to break out of our animating routines and behaviors, if we hold onto our compulsions because we are afraid of the uncertainty of loss when we do not have them, we will lose the possibility of a plenitude beyond that which we can ask or imagine. If we relinquish our compulsions, if we reject them, we will become open for a life that is vital and fulfilling. The secret is accepting the loss of that which is familiar.

If we look at those people in history who have stood up for peace, for love, for justice, and for truth, we will discover that many of them knew that life does not end in death. Hillesum is one of them. Socrates is another. In his final statement to the court that would condemn him to death, he said, "Death is one of two things. Either it is annihilation, and the dead have no consciousness of anything, or...it is really a change—a migration of the soul from this place to another. Now if there is no consciousness but only a dreamless sleep, death must be a marvelous gain, [for I love to sleep].... If on the other hand death is a removal from here to some other place...beyond the reach of our so-called justice, one will find that there are the true judges...and I should like to spend my time there."[17] Dietrich Bonhoeffer was hanged at the age of thirty-nine. According to tradition, his last words were, "This is the end—for me the beginning."[18]

Let us go back just briefly to the Gospel text. Jesus speaks about the grain of wheat in response to his disciples telling him that some Greeks have come to speak with him. This is a significant moment. It means that his signs, his teachings, and his witness have reached beyond the people of Israel, and there is a movement toward his revelation as the universal savior. It is a moment of opening up, a moment of accepting the movement of life that is far beyond his control. "Now the hour has come," he begins. Now that the Greeks have come, his mission to unite humanity is very much in motion. Faced with this opening up, Jesus, who is human, experiences anguish, "Now my soul is troubled." But he refuses to be afraid. "What shall I say: Father, save me from this hour? But it is for that very reason that I have come to this hour." Life is about being on the precipice, refusing to put up a wall for fear, but trusting in the movement of life that is, as St. Paul writes in his Letter to the Ephesians, "more than we can ask or imagine." At the beginning of the text, Jesus says, that the "hour has come for the Son of man to be glorified." Now he makes clear that this implies a complete loss of identity. "Father, glorify your name!" It is only in the abandonment of himself that new life may be given.

In the following chapter of the Gospel of John, Jesus will demonstrate this when he takes off his robe and washes the feet of his disciples, renouncing his place as the master or teacher and taking up the role of the servant. This movement of abandonment continues until upon the cross he says, "'It is fulfilled'; and bowing his head he gave up his spirit." (John 19:30, NJB)

Most of us will not face death in such a drastic way. But all of us will experience the loss that accompanies change and evolution. Will we strive to hold onto control, to hold onto our life as we know it? Or will we be able to accept change, to accept the risk of humiliation, suffering, and anguish? In the above Gospel text, Jesus implies that we must become servants, ready to accept loss, ready to give up our lives, ready to follow without knowing where we are going. Joseph Jaworski says something similar in his intriguing book on leadership, *Synchronicity*. He says that even more radical than the movement right now to become "servant leaders," we must learn to be servants to life; not seeking to control, but seeking to harmonize.

What have been your disappointments, your worst mistakes that you hardly dare share with anyone? When have you hurt people and felt the uncomfortable prodding of conscience after the fact? When have you been utterly lost and confused? When have you been humiliated or rejected? Has your heart been broken? Have you had dreams that have been destroyed? Have you dared to face those realities, or are you afraid to do so? Fear must awaken us to the possibility of growth. For when we overcome our fear, we will discover the compost of our anguish, and we will discover something new. Death is not the end of everything, for from the greatest of all composts, death, will arise a new life.

CHAPTER FIFTEEN

What Happens When We Die?

Death is discrete. We do not find hundreds of birds on the forest floor when we go for a walk. We do not see piles of deceased insects. The line between death and the new life that springs from it is very thin.

And when humans die, there is discretion. Our family may speak about us at the funeral and among themselves. But at a certain point, friends do not know how to bring it up. A room is swept out and prepared for the next inhabitant. Almost thirty years ago, I was quite sick and spent a period in hospital. I became quite friendly with the woman in the next room, offering her flowers when I had received too many. She was very sweet. One day she was just missing. She had been removed during the night. The message was, "We mustn't speak of death!"

At L'Arche we have lived many deaths. One was an assistant named Felix. We laid out the body in the oratory so that each person who wished could have a moment to say good-bye. Several men from the community went together, including Joseph, who had a walker. "Can I kiss him?" he asked. The assistant responded that yes, he could kiss him if he wanted to. "Oh shit, he's cold!" said Joseph, laughing. "Maman is going to be pretty surprised when I say that I have kissed a dead person!" Maman was the woman in charge of the house where he was living. The group of them went out chuckling.

Although he surely would not articulate it this way himself, as Joseph laughed about death, he laughed about his own disability. He laughed about the vulnerability and powerlessness that is part of being human. And in his laughter, he was able to see that death does not define us. He did not say that he had kissed Felix, but rather "a dead person." Felix is much more than the corpse he left behind, and Joseph is much more than his disability—his identity is not confined to his difficulty walking. As he accepted the reality of death as a part of but not the culmination of a life, he accepted his own disability. When we die, when we let go of something we thought was essential in living, we discover a new authenticity. We discover a life greater than we could have imagined.

At L'Arche we have wonderful celebrations of life where people take turns sharing memories, sharing characteristics, sharing what they will miss now that this person is no longer among us. It is as if we gather together to create a grand portrait, each of us painting our little part of the friendship. There is a lot of laughter because we share honestly even about things that were a bit annoying, a bit ridiculous. And there are tears because we realize that we have lost something. We have lost a space of relationship, something about ourselves that was revealed in our personal friendship. As we come together to witness to that space and to let go of it, we discover a mysterious growth. For in our coming together, there is an encounter with this friend in greater color than each of us alone had ever experienced. We get a glimpse of our friend perhaps as God knows her. Life is never diminished in death, only expanded.

We know this to be true historically. When someone dies for truth, for justice, for peace, for love, their life takes on a new proportion, inspiring people around the world to do the same. This is the mystery of martyrdom. We can have no doubt then that new life is given when we die.

But what happens on the other side? I began thinking about this especially after my niece who was dying asked me if her grandmother had suffered when she died. I said that I didn't think so, that she had died quite peacefully. "What happens?" she wanted to know. And so I drew on my experiences and conversations, as well as passages such as this one from Revelation: "He will wipe away all tears from their eyes; there will be no more death, and no more mourning or sadness or pain. The world of the past has gone" (Revelation 21:4, NJB).

As we discussed earlier, loss is an integral part of life. Life is an evolution of loss opening us up to newness. We lose our spot on the basketball team, and we discover that in playing at a lower level we can enjoy the sport without the pressure of winning. We mess up on an exam, and something is lifted from our shoulders as we face the reality that we are not the cleverest, we are not the most academic. But that does not change who we are fundamentally. In accepting this weakness, we may become more open to others in our class who struggle academically. We experience the end of a relationship, the loss of an intimacy that revealed each of us in a new and beautiful way. It is a terrible rupture. And yet, with time and healing, we may discover new freedom. We may discover that we are not beloved just because our partner loved us. We are fundamentally beloved. There are many examples, but you can see that all of life is an evolution of loss and opening. Thus death, which is the ultimate loss, must also be the ultimate opening.

What happens when we die? I believe that we go into a sleep. And then there is an awakening in light. This light is so peaceful and so glorious that when we awake, it is an incredible moment of rejoicing. Is this light God? We are not sure. Perhaps it is a reflection of God. After all, we are not quite ready for a face-to-face or a heart-to-heart encounter. But it is clear that we are welcome here, and we are not alone. There is the feeling of being wrapped up in something wonderfully cozy. There is a deep experience of inner peace.

In the midst of that beauty, that relief and comfort, there is a question: What is going to happen now? Perhaps because we are wondering, searching a little, there is the feeling that in this light, there is a presence. We catch a glimpse of a face. There is a meeting. It is not a union, but there is a relationship. God is not just this light, but a presence, a person. Suddenly I discover that I am loved by this person.

My niece asked me, "What about the fact that I am not a Christian?" I said, "That doesn't matter! You were so good to that immigrant family down the road, you cared for them and loved them. That is all that is important."

It seems to me that to know that we are loved so deeply and so simply would lead to a deep sadness and guilt. How can it be that I am loved? So often I have rejected life, I have failed to be open to life, I have tried to take control myself. So often I hurt people, I have failed to acknowledge their beauty, I have failed to bring them the same sense of peace and belonging that I now feel. I cannot deserve this love! This is a moment of inner pain, even agony. The Church has called it purgatory, which is like purging. All of those moments when we crushed life by failing to witness to the truth, by failing to accept one another, come back. And we are full of guilt and shame to be before this presence of God because we have been so ugly.

Suddenly the face comes back, or perhaps we look up from the depths of our humiliation and see in God a look of tenderness, incredible tenderness. "You are precious in my eyes...and I love you" (Isaiah 43:4). Suddenly, I know that I am loved as I am, *in* my poverty. God knows how weak I am, how many times I have messed up, how I have failed to love, how I have rejected the love of others. And somehow I am loved not *despite* my poverty, but in my poverty. I am forgiven. I imagine that we will burst out laughing. It is all too much to behold, too much to understand. God simply loves us, delights in our littleness, and meets us in our weakness and vulnerability. Everything is upside down; nothing is as we expected. Before the infinite mercy that is God, all the waste of my life becomes compost. It is a moment of wonderful happiness, happy to be myself, happy to know that others are beloved, happy to be a small part of the human body—a little grain of sand on the immensity of God's shore, but so important, so precious, just as every grain is precious.

This is the moment of freedom, here, where we experience God as forgiveness. What does freedom mean? There is freedom *from*. Here in God's mercy, we are freed from the guilt and agony of our past. We are freed from the uncertainty of who we are, freed from the nagging feeling that fundamentally we are sinners, we are unworthy, we are full of hate and despised by others. We are freed from anguish because in God's presence our deepest identity is confirmed. I am beloved.

There is also freedom *to*. So long as we have anguish, we are unable to give ourselves entirely to love. There is something about us that we must keep hidden, that we must protect. But here there is nothing hidden, there is no protecting ourselves. All of us, our strength and our poverty, is gathered together, and God confirms that we are beloved. Here in God's mercy, we are freed to assume this identity of belovedness; we are free to give ourselves entirely to love.

There is the realization that we are an integral part of a body, united with all the diversity that is humanity. It is a revelation of my *unique* belovedness. The body is not whole without me. Nor is the body whole without you, for each of us is essential. We are freed from all jealousy, we are free to accept the beauty of every person, aware of our individual significance to the body as a whole. This is part of the folly of God's forgiveness: the realization that even those who seemed cruel or worthless, that they too are part of this body. God's mercy is infinite, set only upon gathering us all together.

After we have gotten over the folly of God's forgiveness, we long to know God intimately, to desire God. The place of desire is the place of purification. Everything else begins to melt away. Those things that once defined us—the need to be the best, the most special, the need to win—all the things that we assumed to be essential to who we are, fade in light of this relationship with the One who knows us as *beloved*. We burn to meet this one, to know God intimately. We have met God, we have had an experience of God, but we long to be closer, to *dwell* with God, to love God fully and to be fulfilled in that relationship. The place of desire is painful, for desire without fulfillment is pain. But it is the pain of hope, for we have been freed from the doubt that we are worthy to be in God's presence. To be without doubt is to have confidence— and desire with confidence is hope.

Our desire becomes greater and greater, intensifying until suddenly the door opens or the veil drops away. We are in the arms of God, gathered right into the heart of the one who loves us and whom we love. The final division is overcome. The finite becomes infinite; the end becomes eternal. We become one with the one who *is* love, and in this unity we will continue to discover the beginning and end of all things, we will continue to discover the fruitfulness of our weakness. We will not be spectators; we will be actors in the drama of the infinite, life flowing from us in a glorious fount of oneness, giving and receiving life in full.

CHAPTER SIXTEEN

Why Are We Here?

John writes in his first letter, "My dear friends, let us love one another, since love is from God and everyone who loves is a child of God and knows God" (1 John 4:7, NJB). Just as God's love reveals our deepest identity, so do we, by our loving presence, reveal one another. Remember that we *are* in relationship, and so we are here to live in community because this is the fullest way of *being*.

What is community? We can look to our first experience of being part of a group of people: the experience of family. A family is a little bit like a community. We are bonded together by flesh and blood. We may have a similar vision, a similar way of approaching the world, but in fact each is seeking liberty in some ways. A family eventually opens up as children leave home, as parents get older, as grandchildren come along. So a family is a very special grouping of people, but it is not quite the same as a community.

Our next experience might be a close group of friends. As we begin to branch out from the circle of our family, we will form friendships with people that we are attracted to, people that have something in common with us. We share interests, we are studying the same thing, we have common passions and perhaps even angers. Somewhere, we are the same, and we have a feeling that to be together is beautiful. This is something similar to how Jesus's disciples started to be gathered:

Peter and his brother Andrew, James and his brother John, and Philip, who then calls his friend Nathanael. We can see that the first six disciples had a lot in common. They were a group of friends!

They also had a common mission, which was to follow Jesus. In the same way, a group of friends might realize that the passions, angers, and interests that they share comprise a common vision, a desire to change or liberate the world in some way, to show that it is possible to live a little more truthfully, a little more lovingly, a little more justly. In time, other people who we never imagined being friends with might join us because they share in our vision, our dream of living something new. Jesus's disciples also become more diverse. There is Matthew, who was a tax collector; Thomas; Simon, who was part of a group called the Zealots; Jude; and Judas. The group was evolving, no longer simply a group of friends, but disciples.

What we are seeing is that community is more than a group of close friends. There is something about inviting in people who are very different from ourselves but who share a common desire. The disciples were very diverse, but they were united because each was living a response to Jesus's call.

We might say that a community is a unity of love, born from the desire for a common mission. The disciples discover that they are bonded to Jesus, which means that they are bonded to one another in love. There are two fundamental aspects here: love and mission. The realization of these is why *we* are here together.

Mission

Let us look first at mission, and we will come back to love later. There are many kinds of mission. Think about the communities that you are part of: What is your mission? A school community has the mission of educating young people. An artistic community such as a theater company or a choir may have the mission of creating thought-provoking or beautiful performances that touch hearts and minds. Another community might have a mission of serving the poor, working for peace, advocating for human rights, or of environmental steward-ship. A community may also have the mission of praying in the world, of maintaining that quiet proximity to God for all of humanity. What is important is that the mission has something to do with the revelation of truth. There are many possibilities of mission because truth is multi-faceted. There are many ways in which it can be revealed.

Some corporations would like to become more like communities. There is a clear fruitfulness when people are passionate about the work that they are doing and the people that they are doing it with. There is a willingness to engage, over and above the typical job. But I wonder whether an oil company, whose mission is profit and the extraction of an extremely polluting resource, will ever become a community? In fact, whenever profit becomes part of the mission, we can see that there is a deviation from the truth, and it is unlikely that a true community will flourish.

There must be clarity in the mission so as to maintain unity, a continual articulation of the truth that has brought us together. Sometimes this can lead to some difficult situations. Within the first year of opening L'Arche, I picked up someone in my car who was homeless. His name was Gabriel, and he needed a place to stay for a little while, so I invited him to come to L'Arche. At first it was fine, but soon conflicts erupted with Raphael and Philipp, the two men with intellectual disabilities with whom I was living. I realized that I had to make a decision. Either L'Arche was a home where *anyone* who needed a place to stay for a little while would be welcomed, or it was a home particularly for people with intellectual disabilities. I had to ask Gabriel to leave.

These can be very painful decisions. You see, if Gabriel had come with a desire to help create a home with Raphael and Philippe at the heart, there may not have been a problem. Our communities are full of an enormous diversity of people! But our diversity is united by a deep respect for people with disabilities and a commitment to the truth that they have an important gift to bring to the world. Today, L'Arche exists in thirty-five countries around the world! A mission that is founded in truth will unite people who are very different. This is because truth resonates with each of us, the way that Jesus's call resonated with each of his disciples. Unity is never about becoming the same. It is about deepening our unique calling, which ultimately leads us to discover a fundamental oneness in our humanity. Unity is about freedom because we are each living in truth and, as Jesus says, "the truth will set you free" (John 8:32, NJB).

Authority

To be grounded in truth is one of the essential qualities of living authority in community. A community that is unclear in its mission, that is full of conflict, oppression, and revolt, is a community where fears and ambitions are taking the place of truth and love. Authority is about living together in peace.

What is the first thing that comes to mind when you think of authority? Often authority is perceived as "doing what you are told," as enforcing laws and expectations. When we think of authority, we might think of teachers, parents, the government, workplace supervisors, police officers, or judges. We automatically link authority with strength and power. Authority seems to be the imposition of structures, of normality.

But authority first and foremost is grounded in truth. It is about helping people to be on the right track, listening to their consciences, growing in their sense of *I am*, and discovering how beautiful they are. Authority is about growth.

We already know about authority from looking at other types of community, even if we have not yet spoken about it specifically. At school, authority is lived by the teacher who treats his students with respect and care, listening to them, helping them to trust in their intuitions and curiosity. It is about helping children to see that they are important and precious. In a family, the parents have the same role to play, helping their children to discover that they are unique—not unique like everyone else, but unique *with* everyone else—uniquely beloved. Parents must help their children to discover their personal conscience. This means asking their opinions on things and listening seriously, never ridiculing or contradicting them, but, if necessary, asking the right questions that lead to truth and love.

A mother I know told me that her daughter had learned in school about the dangers of smoking cigarettes. When she came home, she expressed her concern to her mother. "I want you to stop smoking, Mom. It isn't good for you, and I don't want you to get sick." Rather than make up some excuse or tell her daughter not to worry, this mother stopped smoking. "I realized that I could not expect my daughter to listen to my advice and concern later, should she begin drinking or using drugs."

Authority is about mutuality insofar as we are all human; we all have a conscience, the presence of God within us. Each of us has the capacity to know what is right and what is wrong. It is about helping one another to be faithful to conscience, to grow in truth. It is about helping each person to awaken and form their capacity to be men and women of conscience, as we have spoken about in an earlier chapter. Authority can only be lived when we love people, when we have the desire that they grow into their unique beauty, that they grow to be themselves.

I was speaking with a group of young people who had been involved with drugs, asking them why they had started, listening to what they had experienced. I asked, "What was your parents' reaction?" One man answered, "They were furious." What was your response to their anger? "Monsieur," he said to me, "my father is an alcoholic." His eyes were angry and defiant. What right did his father have to criticize or to question his son's behavior when he could not control his own? To live authority, we must always be faithful to the truth. That is not to say that his father could not help his son unless he himself had cleaned up. I wonder what would have happened if the father had been open about his struggle and said, "Son, look at me. I am caught in a spiral of addiction that has taken control of my life. I love you and I do not want you to become like me." This is probably what was hidden deep behind the father's anger and rejection of his son. To live authority is to be willing to accept our own vulnerability, to live with fidelity to the truth.

In a community, there are some people that have positions of authority. The community will have a leader, for example, and a council who with the leader determines laws and structures that help each person to live out the mission. These might include the way that a day is structured so that there is time allocated to work and to rest, specific meal times, and the distribution of tasks and responsibilities. It might involve even codes of conduct, acceptable ways of speaking, and so on. Laws are about helping each person to deepen in their understanding of and engagement with the mission.

This can be hard to accept. When we are young and questioning the world, it is hard to believe that laws can serve to bring us toward the truth. Churches have many rules; for example, rules about who can receive communion, rules about marriage and divorce, rules about sexual relationships, rules about liturgy. Sometimes the rules seem overwhelming and restrictive. But part of being in the Church, part of being in any community, is learning discipline and obedience. Discipline is to be like the disciples, daring to follow, trusting that even if we do not yet see why a law is important, it will be revealed in time. As Jesus says to Peter, "What I am doing you do not know now, but afterward you will understand" (John 13:6). Discipline is about following an example. "If I then, you Lord and Teacher, have washed your feet, you also ought to wash one another's feet...love one another; even as I have loved you." (John 13:14, 34). Discipline is about strengthening our bodies, about developing our minds and our capabilities.

It might seem as though there is a contradiction here. After all, we have spoken quite a lot about vulnerability and accepting weakness. Discipline is to help us live our weakness and vulnerability—which is to live our humanity—without fear. Those who are involved in nonviolent movements must train for a long time so as to disarm their hearts, to free themselves of any fears that might compel them to retaliate. Obedience is about listening, stemming from the root words *ob*, meaning "before," and *audiere*, meaning "listen." It is about a soccer team listening to a coach who tells them to run laps or do fitness. It is not much fun, but it will lead toward greater possibilities on the playing field. It is about listening to parents or friends who might tell us not to smoke. We have not yet had an experience of cancer, so it is hard to fully understand *why* this rule exists. But in time, we come to see the wisdom of it. When we are subjugated to laws, we do right to ask questions, to seek the truth that they reveal. But we must also remember that wise people have put them in place. The laws of the Church have been hundreds, even thousands, of years in the making and they are there to guide us toward a deeper relationship with God.

Having said this, the Vatican holds councils where cardinals and lay people, people who are wise, come together to discuss the relevance and function of these laws in the world today. What if a man has AIDS? Should he use a condom? How can we welcome faithful and devout men and women who have felt rejected by the Church because of their sexual orientation? How can the Church be present to people who have had a divorce? These are very difficult and important issues.

When laws are challenged, there are some who clamp down, who become more conservative, who seek to hold fast to traditions for fear that the Church's identity will disappear. Others try to argue for laws to be changed to include all possible exceptions. Neither reaction is very conducive to the growth in unity that the Church is working toward. To hold onto structures in such a way that they are no longer relevant to the people who make up the Church is a denial of reality. On the other hand, an exception cannot be legalized simply because it is an exception, an allowance made in very special cases. We need firm laws so that we can discern whether to allow a deviation from it or not.

The only way to bring these groups together is to come back to the truth that unites us: that Jesus came to Earth to make known to us in his flesh the abundant love that God has for His people. The Church is in motion toward this vision of unity in love. Thus there is wisdom in graduality, helping people to discover the laws that have been developed over thousands of years, not in order to prescribe their relationship with Jesus, but to encourage it and help it grow. This is how the Church is called to live authority: not by strongly enforcing rules, but by asking questions. Another word for this is accompaniment. When we are young, we need to be accompanied by people who have experienced more than we have, who are further along the road to wisdom, who care for us and desire our freedom. Unfortunately, many people do not feel that they are able or worthy to accompany others. But often it is very simple; it is about trusting in and helping to witness to the presence of Jesus in each person and helping others to discover this themselves.

It all comes down to the authority that Jesus lives, which is the authority of love.

There was a young woman who lived in one of our communities in Canada. She—like many who come—had never lived in a community before nor had much experience with people with disabilities. She was a brilliant assistant, getting on well with each one in the house, seeking true relationships rather than just assisting; she was a wonderful source of life. And she too was growing for being here. After being with us for about four months, she unexpectedly became pregnant. Being quite young and not yet having gone to university or entered into professional life, she and her boyfriend did not feel ready to welcome a family. However, I think that it surprised her how difficult the decision of aborting was. Not having any religious upbringing, she might have thought that the elimination of a few cells would not be a big deal. When it was a reality, though, she was painfully aware that she was denying the miraculous, if unexpected, gift that is life. There is no doubt that abortion is something evil. But was this young woman evil? How about her boyfriend? Some would be quick to judge, quick to condemn them.

This reminds me of the eighth chapter of the Gospel of John. "The scribes and the Pharisees brought a woman who had been caught in adultery, and placing her in the midst they said to him, 'Teacher, this woman has been caught in the act of adultery. Now in the law Moses commanded us to stone such. What do you say about her?'" It is a horrible choice. Either Jesus states his agreement with the law, and the woman will be killed; or he speaks against the violence, and the Pharisees have "some charge to bring against him." Jesus does not answer at first. He crouches and begins to write on the ground. They insist he answer, and so he straightens up and says very simply, "'Let him who is without sin among you be the first to throw a stone at her.' And once more he bent down and wrote with his finger on the ground. But when they heard it, they went away, one by one, beginning with the eldest, and Jesus was left alone with the woman standing before him. Jesus looked up and said to her, 'Woman, where are they? Has no one condemned you?' She said, 'No one, Lord.' And Jesus said, 'Neither do I condemn you; go, and do not sin again.'" (John 8:3–11)

Authority is to remain uncompromisingly on the side of life, which is the side of truth and love, of justice and of freedom. And it is to call upon others to do the same. Jesus asks the scribes and Pharisees to be attentive to their own conscience, and to reorient themselves toward the truth. He helps them to discover freedom from the vicious cycle of death that they had created. And then he turns to the woman and does the same, confirming that there is in her the capacity to live truthfully and without sin. He affirms her, helping her to continue to grow to the fullness of her humanity and to freedom.

At L'Arche, rather than judge the young assistant, it was evident that we had to confirm for her in a thousand little ways that she was a beloved child of God. Not to do so might have caused the destruction of two lives—that of her baby and her own—were she to be overwhelmed by guilt and shame. We live authority when we realize that we have within us the capacity to heal the anguish of those around us by the power of our loving presence.

Truth, revealed by the mission and quality of love, are the foundation of community. We live authority by embodying these, being a presence of truth and love, creating spaces for others to grow.

Love

A community can grow from unity in mission or from unity in love. That is to say, a group of friends may realize that they can change the world in some little way by being together. In the same way, a group of people may be gathered together for a common purpose, and over time they realize that they enjoy one another's company, that they look forward to meetings because they are happy to spend time together. A community is united by mission and by the *quality of love* that is lived.

Love is about being concerned for one another. On a soccer team or in a theater group, the members may not care too much about one another. They may enjoy playing together. They may respect the talent of each actor. But when the play is over, when the season is through, each goes their separate way. People united by a mission may become a community by seeing the life that comes when there is real concern for one another, when there is love. We have talked about the nature of love. It means that we are patient with one another, and kind, that we are not jealous but appreciate each as an important and unique part of our community. We do not live competitively with one another, but truthfully. The quality of love in a community is realized in the little moments of a day. It is about asking how you are and really wanting to know. It is about missing someone when they are not there. The quality of love is realized in the way we look at one another at the table, the way we laugh as we wash dishes, the way we delight in the way each person is growing into his or her beautiful unique self.

As we live in community, we will come to see that there is a convergence of the mission and the quality of love. It becomes clear that an integral part of our mission is to reveal to the world that people who are very different can live happily together. L'Arche is a good example of this. Our mission is to "make known the gifts of people with intellectual disabilities, revealed through mutual transforming relationships; foster an environment that responds to the changing needs of our members, whilst being faithful to the core values of our founding story; engage in our diverse cultures, working together toward a more human society."[19]

The truth revealed is that people with intellectual disabilities have a particular gift for bringing people together, inviting us on a journey of human transformation when we are in relationship with them. In a community, the mission is implicit with a desire to give life. Part of mission, therefore, is to care for one another, to be in relationship with one another. If we were simply there to competently provide food and shelter, there would be nothing extraordinary in what we are living. And so part of our mission is to love one another, to show that people who are so different can live happily and peacefully, growing in love, growing in our humanity. Whether the mission is education or charity, environmental or humanitarian (although it is incorrect to assume that these are completely independent from one another), community transmits a message of the beauty and value of every human being, and of the viability of peace.

We can now say that a community is a group of people drawn together by caring for one another and by their common mission, drawn together by love and by truth. We can begin to see that each person is there because somehow, in following their conscience—which guides each of us toward truth, love, justice, and peace—they have discovered unity in their difference. Each has been called, just as the disciples were called.

However, let us not get carried away in idealistic illusions of community. Living in community is not easy. The closer we get to one another, the more dramatic small annoyances become, the more agonizing the behavior of another, and the more our own anguish surfaces. We can become competitive or angry, protective or jealous. Community life can help us discover walls of fear and hatred that we never knew existed. This is the challenge of living together, but it is also an invitation, a knock at the door. For as we face our fears, we come to terms with the reality of our human anguish. As we free our heart from fear and hatred, we become open to greater love. We learn to accept our own belovedness, and we learn, as Jesus invites us, to love our enemies. Community is a school of the heart, an education in peace, where we become more whole, more open to difference, more loving.

Growth begins with the conflicts and tensions that arise when we live together. Jesus's disciples bickered among themselves: "'Who is greatest in the Kingdom of Heaven?' So [Jesus] called a little child to him whom he set among them. Then he said, 'In truth I tell you, unless you change and become like little children you will never enter the kingdom of Heaven…the one who makes himself as little as this little child is the greatest in the kingdom of Heaven'" (Matthew 18:1–4, NJB). Jesus says that the role of community is to help us become like children, to accept our littleness and vulnerability, to become like Jesus himself. "'Anyone who welcomes one little child like this in my name welcomes me.'… 'If your hand or your foot should be your downfall, cut it off and throw it away.'… 'See that you never despise any of these little ones'" (Matthew 18:5, 8, 10, NJB). One thing revealed here is the role of the weakest in our communities, the children, the ones on the periphery, the ones that we would neglect and oppress. They cannot compete; they will never be the best. When we enter into a relationship with them, when we seek reconciliation, we discover freedom from the rat race that can arise in social groupings.

Almost more significantly, however, Jesus is saying that within each of us is the presence of a little child, the presence of God, vulnerable and knocking at the doors of our hearts. The challenge is even within ourselves to "welcome" and "never despise" this presence, but to rid our hearts of the hatred and fears that keep us closed, that destroy the little voice within us. We must be faithful to the little ones in our community and to the little one inside our own hearts, calling us to grow in love.

Forgiveness

Growing in love implies growing toward a vision of unity. The reality is that in community, there are many breakages. Reality, remember, is divided. The disciples show that we can begin to compare ourselves to one another. Perhaps preferences arise, or we seek to avoid one another at all costs. We might start to accuse one another of failing to live the mission. We might disagree over interpretations of the law or the precision with which it is observed. Sometimes tensions can become so acute that we must separate from one another. This has happened in the Church multiple times. It has happened in religious orders, political parties, and even music groups (think of the Beatles). Sometimes, separation happens quite naturally, and both groups find new life with a little space. Gradually, they may come into a renewed relationship. Other times, tensions can lead us to hurt one another, to say something cruel, or even to be physically violent as we try to enforce our way of being and resist oppression. Examples of this can be petty. One man in my community finds it excruciatingly annoying that a woman he lives with takes a long time putting away her table napkin, but will not let anyone else do it for her. Every once in a while, he gets so frustrated he grabs it viciously as she shrieks in rage. The relationship is broken. He must then extend a hand to her in a gesture of forgiveness, and she must accept his hand.

Other examples are much more dramatic. The ongoing conflict in the West Bank is one of the most horrifying witnesses to the unwillingness to forgive. For decades, Israelis and Palestinians have traded violence, each seeming to think that they will eventually cause the other to flee or cow in defeat. And yet the vision of God for humanity is a great coming together. Perhaps some people get a thrill from violence, but the vast majority of us do not like to live in conflict. We are tired of warfare and are much more interested in living together in peace than in seeking revenge. Within each of us is the desire, which is God's desire, to realize our oneness.

Restorative justice is an approach to addressing criminal action that is rooted in this vision. It implies the restoration of that which has been broken, the relationship between human beings. The process varies from country to country of course, but the idea is to bring together criminal and victim—or the family of the victim—so that the truth may be brought to light, the truth of the pain caused as well as the truth that the offender and the victim are people. Restorative justice is about humanizing each person, which is the beginning of forgiveness. It is a radical form of justice in the sense that it brings all those affected back to the roots of our common humanity, to the reality that, whatever our actions, we are all human, we are all hurt and in need of healing.

Forgiveness is not something external or comparable to a simple economic exchange. For all parties, forgiveness implies an interior journey. As we read earlier, Etty Hillesum writes, "The rottenness of others is in us, too.... I really see no other solution than to turn inward and to root out all the rottenness there. I no longer believe we can change anything in the world unless we have first changed ourselves."[20]

A seized napkin is much easier to forgive than seized land. But the process of reconciliation is not dissimilar. Dr. Elisabeth Kübler-Ross detailed some steps in the grief process that might help us to understand the process of forgiveness more thoroughly. After all, loss and grief imply a division or separation, as does hurt and the need for reconciliation.

The first step is denial. From one side or even both sides, there can be passivity, a blockage with regards to the pain sustained because we have not been able to come together. "If she would just get the message and let me put away her napkin, there would be no need for reconciliation!" Sometimes denial can make separations seem like chasms so wide that we forget there is anything on the other side. We do not even see the need for forgiveness.

I once accompanied a young woman on a retreat who, I realized as she spoke to me, had a terrible mistrust and animosity toward men. As we spoke, I wondered about her original relationship with a man: her father. "I hate my father," she told me. He was a teacher at a Catholic school, honored by everyone. But when he came home from work, he would lock himself up in his study, not even coming out to eat with his family or spend time with his daughter. Underneath this woman's hatred of men was a little girl who had never had a chance to forgive her father for not being there. In a way this woman was caught in denial because she did not even seem aware of the need for forgiveness.

This woman also seemed to have been moving into the second step, which is anger. Although she was not yet able to make the connection between her animosity toward men and her relationship with her father, she *was* angry with him. Anger is important. It shows us that there is something amiss in our community; there is a conflict that we can explore in order to find wholeness and a deeper unity. We cannot live in anger forever. It is terribly disagreeable and tiring, like a sickness. And so anger can awaken us to the urgency of reconciliation.

In the more typical system of justice, the need for reconciliation can take on a form that resembles the third step in dealing with grief: bargaining. Rather than the offender shaking hands with the victim, he is given time in jail, a fine, or a sanction, as if this is a reasonable exchange for their action. This is the method taken by the Canadian government with regards to residential school survivors (as we spoke of earlier). By filing allegations of abuse, survivors were offered varying sums of money as compensation for the pain inflicted by government policy and the participation of Churches. But most survivors find little satisfaction from receiving a lump sum; it does not address the flagrant division that still exists between Canadian First Nations and those of immigrant descent who settled in Canada later. It does not help either side to begin a journey of "weeding," of clearing their hearts to be able to face the other.

With the failure of bargaining to bring about healing, parties may be locked into a feeling of powerlessness. Depression is the fourth step.

"Reconciliation just isn't possible." I met a Rwandan woman whose entire family—seventy-five people in all—had been assassinated. "Everyone is talking about forgiveness and reconciliation," she told me, "But I just can't! I'm not ready." She could not imagine ever having the capacity to find healing. "But do you want *them* to be killed?" I asked. "No!" she quickly replied. "There has already been too much death." Although she felt unable to forgive, this woman had already started along the path by freeing herself of vengeance. We might even say that she was moving into the fifth step, which is acceptance. This is not about accepting the crime that has been committed so as to avoid conflict (this would greatly impede our human growth). Acceptance is about beginning to see the humanity of the one who has hurt us, or of the one whom we have injured. It is about accepting that we are all part of one human family and that we too must find it in us to love.

Forgiveness takes time. It is a journey, a process of "weeding out the seeds of hatred" so that we can look at our enemy and see a brother or a sister. To even begin this work, we must have a sense of our own belovedness, of the presence of God within us working in us to do "more than we can ask or imagine" (Ephesians 3:20, NJB). I heard a story of a woman was convicted because of a false witness for a crime that she had not committed. While in jail, she had an encounter with Jesus that helped her discover she was fundamentally beloved and precious. The religious sister who was accompanying her suggested that maybe in this context of healing, they could approach the question of forgiveness. She reacted negatively: "Absolutely not!" There was no way she was ready to forgive. What this man had done was too cruel, too hurtful. "But," she said, "I pray that God will forgive him. I know that I cannot, but somehow he must discover the evil in his heart, the evil that is crushing what is beautiful there. I cannot reveal this to him, but God can."

Forgiveness is about believing in and revealing the humanity of our enemy. If we come back to the example of the woman who carried deep resentment for her father, I might have asked her about her grandfather, to help her to see that her father had also been wounded. Forgiveness begins with compassion, with opening our hearts to the humanity and woundedness of our enemy. It is also to see that violence is committed in a context. People become slaves to a culture of violence, ensnared by the trivialization of violence, so that they are hardly aware of their actions.

A book by Hannah Arendt, called *Eichmann in Jerusalem: A Report on the Banality of Evil,* came out in 1963. It describes the trial of a Nazi colonel and one of the main organizers of the killing of millions of Jews. As a Jewish woman who had herself fled the Nazi regime, Arendt's conclusions are quite strong. She writes that the colonel did not seem particularly bloodthirsty, nor deranged, nor even anti-Semitic. Rather, he was someone who had an identity of following orders without question. She calls this the "banality of evil." If the structures within which one functions are predisposed to extreme violence, it can be very easy to act inhumanely. We can see this occurring in lesser ways in our own communities. At school or in our workplace, it becomes normal to tease a particular person. No one really *hates* that person, but a derogatory rhetoric has become normal. In the United States, it was normal to have black slaves. Certainly, there were hundreds of plantation owners who were not evil people, but they never thought to question the status quo. In Canada, it was government legislation that First Nations people be taken from their families and sent to residential schools—stripped of their culture, their language, and their land. Many of the people working at the schools, participating in evil, did not think twice about their actions because it was normal. How do we come to forgive in such situations?

In a mysterious way, offender and victim are not very different from one another. Each is enclosed in a world of hatred and violence. Whether we have hurt someone, or whether we ourselves have been injured, we must find the grace with which to touch the hand of the other. Forgiveness is a road toward freedom from anger, from hatred, from shame, and from vengeance. We can accept this journey only when we realize the extent to which we are imprisoned by our refusal to work toward reconciliation. Freedom implies being stripped of our image, of all pretense and context, stripped down to the fundamentals of our humanity. Freedom means exposing only the truth, for the truth will set us free.

Forgiveness is a gift of God, a grace given when our hearts are prepared, when we have freed ourselves and the world of "every atom of hate" within us, when we have been able to empty ourselves so as to receive each other. The ultimate example of forgiveness is of course Jesus at his crucifixion. The Gospel of Luke tells that as his hands and feet were nailed to the cross, he said, "Father, forgive them; they do not know what they are doing" (Luke 23:34, NJB). In the Gospel of John, we read of five stages in his emptying out of himself. First a sign is placed above Jesus's head: "Jesus the Nazarene, King of the Jews" (John 19:19, NJB). It is the stripping of Jesus's identity as the Messiah, the Son of God, human and one with all of humanity. Next, they strip him of all his clothing. Jesus is physically naked, baring all of his human vulnerability, all that God assumed when the Word became flesh. After this, Jesus sees his mother at the foot of the cross with John the disciple standing by. "'Woman, this is your son.' Then to the disciple he said, 'This is your mother'" (John 19:26, NJB). Jesus offers his mother to the church, which is to open up his family to include each of us, giving even the most intimate of his relationships for the unity of God's people. "After this, Jesus knew that everything had now been completed" (John 19:28, NJB). He is utterly emptied out, vulnerable, and weak. All that is left to him is the possibility of relationship.

When we have weeded out all the hatred within us, when we are truly ready to face our enemy, it will be in vulnerability—stripped down to an identity of being human and nothing more. In forgiveness, our title or function is of little importance. Our exterior image and the ways in which we cover our weakness have been stripped away. Our identity is not as someone's daughter or wife, uncle or son. Forgiveness is about loss between human beings: losing face, losing illusions, losing ideals. Forgiveness and reconciliation imply loss. In this poverty, all we have to offer is an invitation to relationship.

Jesus says, "I am thirsty" (John 19:28, NJB). It brings us back to the moment at the well with the Samaritan woman. Jesus, in his utter poverty and nakedness, is calling us simply to be in communion with him. The call of "I thirst" is the also the promise of living water. The soldiers soak a sponge in sour wine, refusing even to respond to this very human cry. "After Jesus had taken the wine he said, 'It is fulfilled'; and bowing his head he gave up his spirit" (John 19:30, NJB). In his utter aloneness, there is completion. And there is the revelation of one last gift, that of the Spirit. Forgiveness implies death, and in that death the giving of new life. Jesus gave up his Spirit, breathing it upon the world. To receive the Spirit, we must become as vulnerable as Jesus. To receive the grace that is forgiveness, we must each come to a point of vulnerability and emptiness.

Jesus tells a parable of two sons and a father. The younger son asks for his share of his inheritance and goes off to pursue a life of extravagance and wastefulness. Soon he had spent it all. To get by, he took on a job at a farm, where he was housed with the pigs, enviously hungering after their cornhusks.

> "How many of my father's hired men have all the food they want and more, and here I am dying of hunger! I will leave this place and go to my father and say: Father, I have sinned against heaven and against you; I no longer deserve to be called your son; treat me as one of your hired men."… While he was still a long way off, his father saw him and was moved with pity. He ran to the boy, clasped him in his arms and kissed him…. Now the elder son was out in the fields, and on his way back, as he drew near to the house, he could hear music and dancing…. He was angry then and refused to go in, and his father came out and began to urge him to come in; but he retorted to his father, "All these years I have slaved for you and never once disobeyed any orders of yours, yet you never so much as offered me so much as a [young goat] for me to celebrate with my friends."… The father said, "My son, you are with me always and all I have is yours. But it was only right we should celebrate and rejoice, because your brother here was dead and has come to life; he was lost and is found." (Luke 15:17–32, NJB)

God is mercy. God is this father who delights when we begin the work of forgiveness. When we turn to God and say, "I cannot live anymore.

I need you to help me," God runs to meet us. We may be like the younger son, broken, vulnerable, coming empty handed, except for the reality of our mistakes. "Forgive me." We may be the elder son, slow to forgive, angry and resentful, unable to make room in his heart for his little brother. God so longs for us to find unity. He comes out to speak to his elder son also, to tell him that they are deeply bonded: "You are with me always and all I have is yours." He longs for his two sons to be gathered into this unity, just as God longs for us to be together in communion with one another.

Forgiveness leads us toward the feast, a wonderful celebration of the life that has been given. As the father says, "Quick! Bring out the best robe and put it on him; put a ring on his finger and sandals on his feet. Bring the calf we have been fattening and kill it; we will celebrate by having a feast" (Luke 15:22–23, NJB).

Forgiveness is about reestablishing our unity. Barriers founded in fear have disappeared, peace is restored, and we are in communion. We all need to forgive, we all need to be forgiven. Forgiveness is the way of community, a road we are taught to walk with greater ease, greater openness. We are always learning to forgive, which is to learn to love. Forgiveness leads us toward a feast, a celebration, because new life has been given. We have rediscovered a son, a daughter, a brother, a sister. Forgiveness is a journey toward the revelation of our fundamental oneness.

Why are we here? We are here to build community. Why is this so important? Community is a place of growth and transformation, a place where we grow to be more fully and freely ourselves in relationship with others. Community is where we discover the fundamental and life-giving tension of freedom and belonging. This is the tension of the body of humanity; you do your part, I do mine, and at the same time we are united. We belong to one body, and yet we must have the freedom to fulfill our unique role, to take our rightful place. In a community, we belong to one another, we belong to the mission, and yet we cannot be enslaved by the structures and relationships. Each one must be able to live the mission according to his or her conscience, to love mutually. In community, we discover that freedom and belonging are not opposites; to grow in freedom brings us closer together as we discover our belonging to a common humanity, our belonging because we are beloved. And to grow in belonging brings us to greater liberty. As Bonhoeffer writes, "I am thine," and it is this that frees him from his fear and anguish. Community is where we help one another discover that to belong to one another we must each belong to God—and this is the greatest freedom of all.

CHAPTER SEVENTEEN

What Matters In Death? What Matters In Life?

I must not suppress the voice within, call it 'conscience', call it 'prompting of my inner basic nature…. That something in me which never deceives me tells me now: "… Do not fear. Trust that little thing which resides in the heart…testify to that thing for which you have lived, and for which you have to die.[21]

What is "that thing for which you have lived, and for which you have to die"? Without finding a definitive answer, we can read that what matters in life is also what matters in death. There is no separation, for we have seen by now that death is *integral* to life. It is *integral* in this journey of growth, comprising all of our experiences—some wonderful, some difficult, some bearing nourishing fruits, some yielding rich compost. Growth is a journey of loss and gain.

We have been discovering that growth is about overcoming divisions between people, breaking down barriers of fear and hatred. Growth is about becoming a society where, black or white, we are all part of one human family. It is about discovering that we are part of an ecosystem and about growing in concern for its stewardship, for the cleanliness of the air we breathe, for the sustainability of our common resources. Growth is about realizing our interconnectedness. It is about gradually opening our hearts to people who are very different from us, taking time to listen to them and to hear their stories. It is about letting go of our own egoism and becoming open to the other, even to the one who wants to hurt us, and learning to love our enemy. What matters is that we are learning to "trust that little thing which resides in the heart," our inner voice which "never deceives" and guides us to wisdom.

A Journey to Wisdom

Wisdom is not knowledge. It is a way of being, a way of searching for what is true and just in the world. It is about growing toward the origin and the fulfillment of all things, about growing in humility. Those who are wise are free from the need to have power, the need to win, the need to be better than others and to prove themselves. They are open to something that surpasses everything, something that is greater than all of us. Growth in wisdom begins with the acceptance of our poverty, the acceptance that we have much to learn. "Wisdom begins with the sincere desire for instruction" (Wisdom, 6:17, NJB). The wise King Solomon describes how his journey of growth in wisdom began with an encounter, which inspired in him a profound humility and open generosity. He writes, "The spirit of Wisdom came to me. I esteemed her more than scepters or thrones.... I held riches as nothing.... I loved her more than health or beauty.... What I learned diligently, I shall pass on liberally...for she is to human beings an inexhaustible treasure, and those who acquire this win God's friendship" (Wisdom, 7:7–14, NJB). Wisdom is about openness to that which is over and above us, "a breath of the power of God" (Wisdom, 7:25, NJB), urging us to grow. It is to see that life is a journey, beginning with the discovery of Wisdom "sitting at the door" (Wisdom 6:14, NJB), an encounter.

Talking about death in an earlier chapter, we imagined an *encounter* that opened up a deepening journey, a journey of moving toward the embrace of God. It is a moment of intense joy and freedom when, in all our poverty and failings, with all our mistakes and littleness, we know that we are loved. We live something similar at the beginning of our lives. After the tremendous rupture of birth, we are held tenderly against the breast of our mother. This is the birth of *I am*; I am because I am beloved. This moment at our birth and this moment in death are in some ways the same moment—an encounter with God within us, and an encounter with God who welcomes and loves us just as we are. What matters in death, what matters in life, is that we continue to live moments of rebirth, growing from our initial experience of beloved-ness toward our fulfillment. This is the journey to wisdom; this is the journey to oneness with God.

Wisdom is about seeking *communion* with God. Communion is an important word. The first chapter of the Gospel of John says, "In the beginning was the Word, and the Word was with God, and the Word was God" (John 1:1). I understand this to mean that the Word was in *communion* with God. To be in communion means that we have a mysterious experience of becoming one. Jesus invites us to be in communion with him, the Word made flesh. "Whoever eats my flesh and drinks my blood lives in me and I live in that person" (John 6:56, NJB). Communion with Jesus is communion with God, for as Jesus states plainly, "The Father and I are one...the Father is in me and I am in the Father" (John 10:30, 38, NJB). Jesus's prayer is that all people "may be so perfected in unity" (John 17:23, NJB), that all may be gathered in communion with God, and then in communion with one another. Moments of communion give us a taste of what we are moving toward as we grow in love.

Communion

Let us begin by distinguishing between communication and communion. One might think, in this age of e-mail, cell phones, Facebook, and Twitter, that being in communion is something obvious. We can send written messages with the touch of a finger. Hearing the voice of someone thousands of miles away takes no more effort than picking up the phone. News circles the world in minutes. A poorly articulated statement by the Central Bank in the USA can have European stock markets reeling in no time. We are so connected!

Yet, despite social media and other communication tools, we seem to know very little about *communion*. As the Beatles put it, "All the lonely people, where do they all come from?"[22] We aspire to live in one-bedroom apartments, to drive our own cars, to be thoroughly independent. In ways hardly observable, we adhere to an individualistic vision of humanity that is not about communion and can only suggest anguish. Those who teach us about communion are those who are vulnerable and dependent, those who may not have the slightest idea about e-mail or Skype or texting. When we dare to be in relationship with them, they can liberate us from a world of isolation and anguish. Communion is about mutual presence.

Mutual presence simply means that I am with you. I am *because* I am with you, my deepest being is revealed because we are together. Mutual presence implies humility, my sense of self fading into a reality of togetherness. It implies an abandonment of my self, of my preoccupations and reasons not to be there. It is about growing in trust and the freedom to love. Presence is about marveling at the beauty and the brokenness of others, listening to their words, hearing their pain, their joy, and caring about them. Mutual presence is about allowing compassion to grow, revealing our radical togetherness. What does this mean? *Radical* means "root." And so radical togetherness means that we are bound together in the roots of our humanity, growing to fulfillment.

We are bonded because within each of us there is a presence guiding us, a yearning for truth, love, justice, and freedom. Conscience leads us toward communion, toward a realization of the body that encompasses humanity and our place in it. It is about becoming one with the mothers in Calcutta as well as the stockbrokers on Wall Street, for we are all part of a diverse and beautiful human family.

This journey begins with a moment, a taste of communion. This might be a moment like mine with my father when I was thirteen years old, an affirmation of conscience, a sense of *I am* being born. Or it might be an experience of something beautiful: a painting, voices coming together in harmony, bodies moving gracefully, words that seem to come from the very depths of our own soul. We may have a moment of communion within our community gathered to celebrate, to share a meal, or to remember someone dear to us who has died.

We may have a moment of communion when we bear witness to something extraordinary and truthful, something that touches the depths of our hearts and awakens our longing for justice and peace. It might be a moment like when Martin Luther King Jr. spoke of the dream of the black and white people in the United States—a dream of unity, which is the dream of God. Or when Gandhi and hundreds of Indians participated in the Salt March, a nonviolent act of civil disobedience in protest of the oppressive colonial British presence. Their walking touched our own longing, God's longing, for freedom. Moments of communion are moments of birth and of the rebirth of our longing for truth, love, justice, peace, freedom. They orient our searching; they nourish us and encourage us to keep walking.

A moment of communion opens us up to the infinite. We discover that we are called to be in communion with all of God's creation: with the universe, with the sun which gives energy to the plants that feed us, with the stars that shine from the time of our ancestors, with the moon whose orbit moves the great bodies of water on our shorelines. We are becoming one with the creatures that live under this same sky, the great trees, and the vast stretches of desert. This begins with a moment of communion, a moment of wonderment. But then we must grow in it. We seek to learn about the planets and ecosystems in order to expand our knowledge and to deepen our relationship. Communion is not something that we achieve or obtain, it is a moment on a journey that tells us we are moving in the right direction.

Here at L'Arche, there is often a moment of communion after we finish praying as a household. Our prayers are not elaborate. We light a candle, sing a song, perhaps read a short Bible passage. And then each person is invited to confide something in God—something for which they are grateful or a hope, a pain, that they want to share. Some people do not speak, knowing that God sees all that is in our hearts. Then we might hold hands and together pray, "Our Father, who art in Heaven..." Whatever the struggles of the day—the sufferings, pain, imperfections, failings to love of each one—we are gathered as children of God. The prayer is over, but no one rushes to blow out the candle. At this moment, there is nothing else except to be in presence of one another. A warm silence descends; our hearts are united into one heart. This is a moment of communion, a birth or rebirth of our deepest identity.

Our deepest identity is about a yearning for communion. After we are born, our mother holds us tenderly, revealing to us that our body, naked and weak, is precious and beautiful. Our mother looks at us with wonder and adoration, and we know that we are important. It is a look that says, "You are more precious that you dare to believe!" Our fundamental human value, our belovedness and sense of *I am,* is born in that relationship with our mother as we experience *communion* in love for the first time.

I am is not a singular identity but an identity in relationship to another. In the womb, *I am* within my mother. In death, *I am* with God. Archbishop Desmond Tutu describes the word *ubuntu,* which speaks about "the essence of being human…that my humanity is caught up, bound up and inextricable in yours. When I dehumanize you, I inexorably dehumanize myself. The solitary human being is a contradiction in terms."[23] Do you see that this is a very different way of looking at the world than we are used to? Often, we are taught that we are individuals. We pursue our own interests, we seek to maximize our personal benefit, we hope to achieve individual happiness. I might be in relationship with others, but only insofar as there is something in it for me. I might seek to gain knowledge about the stars, the seas, and the wonders of the universe, but only for my personal advancement.

And yet, doesn't this seem like quite a limited view of what it means to be human? So long as we are caught in a world of walls between you and me, so long as we pursue relationships with one another and with the earth for a reason other than communion, we will find ourselves living in anguish.

Anguish

Anguish comes with our first great separation: the rupture of birth. The world is so big! We are small and lost within it. Where do I begin and where do I end? Who am I in this vastness? It is a moment like that of Adam and Eve in the garden, naked and hiding, afraid. There is a movement of life that began in the womb, a movement that means we are changing. In the womb, there is security. And yet, the desire to live pushes us to leave this place of security and we are born. In the security of our mother's arms, we have the same struggle, a biological impulse to grow which leads us away from our mother's embrace as we grow physically and as we become independent. The desire to live is innate and leads us to grow in truth and in love, but it also implies that we will experience anguish.

Anguish, profound loneliness, is what animates our need to win, to be the best. It animates our compulsions. We have spoken before of compulsions; they keep us busy so that we do not have to face our anguish. We may be hooked on Facebook because it gives a sense of sociability. We may binge because somewhere within us there is a sense of emptiness. Or we may deny ourselves something because we are tormented by an impossible ideal and are unable to accept our unique beauty. We may speak quickly and loudly so that we don't have to hear others. We may smoke because it gives us a sense of fraternity and fills our minutes between things. We may work incessantly because unconsciously we feel the need to produce, to prove ourselves, and to win.

Compulsions can lead to addictions. We study until early morning hours all week, cramming so as to get the very best grade, or even to scrape by. Friday night we relieve the pressure with mixed drinks and beer. Saturday night is the same. At first it is one weekend now and again. But quickly it can become every weekend; we can hardly get through a week of classes except for the promise of a weekend of partying. It might even become a beer in the evenings. What I am saying might sound a little drastic, and it could be good to go for a drink with friends on occasion. But if we begin to rely on booze as a solution to our loneliness, there will be no possibility for growth. For our loneliness, our anguish, is the suffering of our desire for the infinite, our insatiable yearning to know God. If we are caught in a cycle of satisfaction from alcohol, drugs, sex, or even work, we will stifle our impulse to grow.

How to free ourselves from compulsions? I am in awe of people who are brave enough to go through the process of recovery. Recovering from an addiction is an extremely rigorous program of spiritual—indeed human—growth. Some of the wisest people in the world are part of Alcoholics Anonymous, working their way through the twelve steps. Let us read them together.

We admitted we are powerless over alcohol and our lives have become unmanageable.

Came to believe that a Power greater than ourselves could restore our sanity.

Made a decision to turn our will and our lives over to the care of God *as we understood Him.*

Made a searching and fearless moral inventory of ourselves.

Admitted to God, to ourselves, and to another human being the exact nature of our wrongs.

Were entirely ready to have God remove these defects of character.

Humbly asked Him to remove our shortcomings.

Made a list of all persons we had harmed, and became willing to make amends to them all.

Made a direct amends to such people wherever possible, except where to do so would injure them or others.

Continued to take personal inventory and when we were wrong promptly admitted it.

Sought through prayer and meditation to improve our conscious contact with God *as we understood Him*, praying only for the knowledge of His will for us and the power to carry that out.

Having had a spiritual awakening as the result of these Steps, we tried to carry this message to alcoholics, and to practice these principles in all our affairs.[24]

Do these steps resonate at all with your own experience? An addiction such as alcohol accentuates the need for growth, but the twelve steps of AA articulate a human journey that is relevant for each of us—a journey of and toward communion, which is liberation from anguish.

Athenagoras, Patriarch of Constantinople, wrote,

> I have waged this war against myself for many years.
> It was terrible.
> But now I am disarmed.
> I am no longer frightened of anything
> because love banishes fear.
> I am disarmed of the need to be right.[25]

He wrote that to be disarmed is no longer to have the need to be right, to disprove others so as to justify one's own argument, to always have more than others, or to possess everything. This is the journey to wisdom. It is about becoming free from fear so that we can listen to our inner voice, the presence of God within us. Growth in love is about accepting vulnerability and accepting reality. It is about forgiveness, fidelity, and helping others to grow. And all of it is done *in relationship* with God "*as we understood him*." It begins with an encounter, with the acceptance of our littleness and our need for relationship "to restore our sanity," which helps us to heal and grow.

We begin to address our anguish when we realize that fundamentally we are not alone. I knew a man struggling with alcoholism who had a grace-filled time of sobriety as he was caring for his cousin, who was also struggling with alcohol. When social services intervened and found a place for his cousin to go through rehab, this man went back to the bottle. He no longer had anyone to care for. We are beings *in communion*. The treasure of our humanity, our belovedness, is revealed in our relationships with others and in our relationship with God, who says to us, "You are my beloved in whom I am well-pleased" (see Mark 1:11).

Fidelity to Growth

Certainty of our belovedness is fragile. That "little thing...within your heart," conscience, is easily stifled. Jesus is vulnerable and weak, knocking at the door. Someone in AA reflected that however many years sober, each person in a meeting was just "one drink away from addiction." What do we need to stay on this path of growth? What must we put in place so that we can be faithful on our journey to wisdom?

Perhaps the most important and the most difficult thing is time. The secret to growth is to take time, to take *your* time to be present and to wonder at the beauty of the universe, the beauty of all those around us, and to truly see the presence of God in all people.

To take time is about *fidelity* to growth. Fidelity is not a word that we use often, but it is very profound in its meaning. Its etymological roots imply *faith* and *trust*. Often as we are growing, we can lose heart. We cannot see what our journey is leading to, we feel discouraged and even skeptical. Fidelity is about maintaining our trust in a "power greater than ourselves." It is about trusting that even when the end is not clear, if each of our steps is oriented toward life, we are going in the right direction.

As I look back at the history of L'Arche, I can see how this has been true. Not even a year after Raphael, Philip, and I began to live together in our little L'Arche house, the director of the Val Fleurie, the local institution where my friend was chaplain, quit. I was asked to take over direction of the institution. This was not at all what I had planned when I moved to France. I had imagined a little house; the Val Fleurie was enormous. I had imagined a small, family-like setting with a few men; the Val Fleurie was home to thirty. Imagine!

And yet nothing could have been more providential! People in the village came to help us, we had the accompaniment of a wonderful psychiatrist, and assistants came and chose to stay. Little by little, the chaos of the institution subsided and we began to form a vibrant community. We learned to love one another; we discovered our mission together as a sign of peace in the world. L'Arche began to grow in ways that I could not have imagined. In 1968 I was asked to give a retreat in Canada to priests, lay people, and religious. It was a beautiful experience, one of communion among all the participants. One of these was a sister from Our Lady's Missionaries. She offered us the community's novitiate and the beautiful grounds around it so that we could start a L'Arche house there. Amazing. L'Arche could begin in Canada! Every founding story follows a similar trajectory, one of being led by Wisdom, by the "breath of…God" toward the realization of God's own desire: a community that is a sign of God's love for humanity. All God asks is that we live in trust and in faith, that we live with fidelity to life.

Fidelity implies commitment. Commitment is not something that comes easily. Looking around today, there are many ways in which commitment has become quite fleeting: people change jobs frequently, they move to different neighborhoods, they do not join political parties or community groups, Church attendance is declining, people are less rooted in their local community and economy, and broken families have almost become commonplace. Commitment means building our houses upon solid ground. Jesus says, "Everyone who comes to me and listens to my words and acts on them…is like the man who, when he built a house, dug, and dug deep, and laid the foundations on rock; when the river was in flood it bore down on that house but could not shake it, it was so well built" (Luke 6:47–48, NJB).

There are three aspects to commitment, to living with fidelity to growth. The first is to come to Jesus, to have the desire for wisdom, the desire for truth, and to be drawn toward love. It is like the disciples who get up and follow Jesus. It is about opening the door to the one who is knocking. The second is to listen, to listen to our little voice, to listen to our experiences, to listen to those who are wise, to those who help us to live in reality. To listen means to welcome the one who knocks at the door, to hear their story, to hear their need. To listen is to hear their invitation, the cry of God. The third is to act upon what we hear. To act is about *respons*ibility—*responding* to what we have listened to, befriending the one whom we have welcomed, and accepting their invitation. Come, listen, act. This is the way of growth.

Rituals of Communion

How do we nourish our commitment to growth, to listening to our inner voice, to our relationship with God? For me personally, it is about attending the Eucharist every day, keeping an appointment with Jesus, an appointment with love. It is intentionally taking time for mutual presence. Somehow, by receiving the body and blood of Jesus, I have a moment each day where *I am* because I am in Jesus and Jesus is in me. There is a physical sense of peace and well-being that is beyond words.

The Eucharist is what I would call a ritual of communion. Rituals of communion give us the courage to keep going. They are not about taking time alone, but about taking time to realize our identity as being in a communion of love. Of course, they are in solitude, but it is an *encounter with love* in solitude. Rituals help us to become free of our fear of anguish because they are an experience of our fundamental belovedness, something that God alone can reveal. They are like food along the way, giving us what we need to continue as well as a taste for what is coming. We need them to grow.

What are your rituals of communion? This is time to *be* in one's body and to have an encounter in stillness with what is *heard, seen, watched, and touched.* Another ritual of communion might be meditating on the word of God, be it in the Bible or another religious text. It is about letting the spirit in the words join us where we are, listening for the wisdom that meets us in the movement of our own journey. Even the same passage read over and over again will speak to us differently every time. This is the mystery of the living Word.

Many people find a quality of communion when they are with people with disabilities, people who live on the street, people who are close to death, people who are struggling, those who are in need of love. This is a quality of communion with the poor. Jesus says:

> I was hungry and you gave me food, I was thirsty and you gave me drink, I was a stranger and you made me welcome, lacking clothes and you clothed me, sick and you visited me, in prison

and you came to see me.... In truth I tell you, in so far as you did this to one of the least of these [brothers and sisters] of mine, you did it to me. (Matthew 25:35–36, 40, NJB)

People who are on the margins call us out of our self-centered existence and remind us of our commitment to growth; they remind us to listen to our inner voice.

Moments of communion may also be moments of beauty. We must take time to write, to paint, to read and appreciate the work of others, to walk in nature, to listen to music, to sing. Appreciating beauty can lead us in some mysterious way to be in communion with the universe; we become aware of something over and above us that we are part of but cannot fully grasp.

Moments of communion nourish our fidelity because they are about a coming back to the source, to the wonderment that led us into a particular way of life. In a marriage, it is essential for the relationship that the couple takes time together. It is in secret shared moments that their love for one another is renewed and sustained. Our commitment to growth must be the same, secret moments of presence with love.

> I hear my love
> See how he comes
>
> …
>
> My love lifts up his voice,
> he says to me
> 'Come then, my beloved,
> my lovely one, come
>
> …
>
> My love is mine and I am his."
> —Songs, 2:8, 10, 16, NJB

So right now, put away this book and take some time for communion. Once I asked a young woman who had recently entered a contemplative order how she prayed. She said that she just sat and waited for Jesus. It doesn't sound too hard, does it? If you are having some trouble, think of a moment when you felt an encounter with love, when you were filled with peace and a deep happiness, a sense of wonder and beauty. Let the feeling of it fill your body. Do not try to put words to your experience, just *be* in it, present, in communion with love.

Beginning

Here we are, the end of a book, the beginning of something new. This book has been about wrestling, about following the invitation to "come and see," about asking questions. We have learned a lot, but I still have many more questions and I hope that you do too. If we have questions, we will continue to journey and we will continue to listen—and that is what this is all about! As I said at the beginning, this is not a book of answers. What I hope, however, is that you have discovered that somewhere in the deepest place of your heart, there is yearning for communion.

There is an inner call which leads all of us to follow truth, love justice, peace, and which guides us toward our human fulfillment. We need a special grace so that we can begin to trust in that call, so that we can live in response to it with confidence and fidelity. Often we describe this sort of journey as spirituality. There are those who will turn away, who will say that they are not particularly spiritual. And yet, it is a human journey. It is about finding the ways of living, the rituals, the moments in the presence of God, that lead us on the road to plenitude in love.

This book has certainly been written with a Catholic bias, but it should not be inaccessible or irrelevant to other denominations or religions. We are all part of one human family, beloved children of God. However, it is important to be rooted in some tradition. Ambiguity or over-inclusiveness often disorients us. It is not by assimilation or adoption of another's customs that we become one, but by deepening our own traditions and discovering that in our difference there is a radical unity. There is oneness in the roots of our humanity, oneness in wisdom.

Our journey to wisdom is not a matter of willpower or strength of character. It is much simpler and much more challenging; we are brought closer to God through the acceptance of our poverty. The most important thing to remember is, "Do not fear. Trust that little thing that resides in your heart. Testify to that for which you have lived and for which you have to die." It is about fidelity and not abandoning an ideal of peace and justice, an ideal of truth and love. It is about losing one's life for the Kingdom of God that is here and that is coming. "Do not fear."

What do we have to fear? Gandhi says it is "that for which you have to die." He does not say, "that for which you *may* have to die." It is inevitable. In the journey toward justice and love, we will experience death. So naturally we become fearful. At the same time, we know that we must give up our lives if we are to find them. We must know the cross if we are to know the resurrection. We must know that loss is integral to growth. We must die to our personal mission and ambitions so that we discover our place in the vision of God: God's mission of uniting the world in truth and love, the mission of peace.

Gandhi's words imply the humility of becoming human, of becoming men and women of peace, justice, truth, and love. Often our dreams of peace, justice, and unity seem impossible, even foolish and idealistic.

We must accept this. But we must never lose faith that they are *becoming* possible, they are *becoming* reality. Every experience of death brings us closer to God, brings us closer to "that for which [we] have lived." We are called to live *hope*. Hope is a way of being that is firmly rooted in reality but moves toward an ideal that is not yet there. Hope is a community, a sign of radical togetherness, a reality of conflict and difference on a journey of forgiveness. Hope is testifying to that which we have *heard*, *seen*, *looked upon*, and *touched*, that which *was from the beginning* and that which is becoming. Hope is giving thanks for the journey that we are on together.

Hannah Arendt (1906–1975). A German and Jewish philosopher, Arendt's documentation of the trial of Nazi colonel Adolf Eichmann, *Eichmann in Jerusalem: A Report on the Banality of Evil,* revealed the institutionalization of violence and the facility with which normal human beings might commit horrendous atrocities.

Dietrich Bonhoeffer (1906–1945). A Lutheran pastor in Germany and author of the spiritual classic *The Cost of Discipleship,* Bonhoeffer was imprisoned for his outspoken resistance to Nazi policies. He was prayerful and composed as he was hanged at Flossenburg concentration camp just weeks before the end of World War II.

Dorothy Day (1897–1980). A journalist and communist activist, Day advocated against the world war, and on behalf of women's rights and civil rights. She became a Catholic and founded with Peter Maurin the Catholic Worker Movement in New York City in 1933. Day was an outspoken witness to nonviolence in her writing, public protest, and lifestyle.

Dekanawidah (The Great Peacemaker) (16th century). Although the spelling of his name and the details of his story vary, Dekanawidah was probably born among the Huron tribe. Joined by Hiawatha, a former warrior, he then delivered the Great Law of Peace to warring nations in central and eastern North America. His Great Law of Peace forms the basis of the Six Nations constitution.

Albert Einstein (1879–1955). Best known for his theory of relativity, Einstein was a pacifist, believing in the capacity of science to bring humanity together. In the interwar period, he was active in various international efforts at scientific cooperation. Moving to the U.S. in the 1930s, he was devastated by the detonation of the atomic bomb and later regretted his early wartime support of the project.

Mohandas (Mahatma) Gandhi (1869–1948). Born in India and trained as a lawyer in London, Gandhi's experience of oppression as an Indian man in South Africa catalyzed his development of *Satyagraha*, "devotion to truth," a way of nonviolent resistance and living peace. He became an important figure in India's movement toward independence, leading through a vision of peace and unity that transcended racial and religious barriers.

Esther (Etty) Hillesum (1914–1943). A Jewish resident of Amsterdam during the Nazi occupation, Hillesum's letters and diaries chronicle her spiritual and intellectual development. She was imprisoned at concentration camps at Westerbork and Auschwitz, where she was killed.

Abdul Ghaffar Khan (Bacha Khan) (1890–1988). A close friend and follower of Mahatma Gandhi, Khan was a man of nonviolence and peace. He helped to lead the participation of Pashtun people, a population in Pakistan and Afghanistan in India's independence movement. In later years, he continued to advocate against the partition of India and Pakistan, and for the unique voice of the Pashtun minority.

Martin Luther King Jr. (1929–1968). A Baptist pastor inspired in part by Gandhi's principles of nonviolence, King became one of the primary leaders of the American Civil Rights Movement and an international icon for social justice. He received the Nobel Peace Prize in 1964 and was assassinated in 1968.

Nelson Mandela (1918–2013). A South African anti-apartheid politician, Mandela served twenty-seven years in prison on charges of attempting to overthrow the government. An international campaign to secure his release was successful in 1990. In 1993, Mandela and President F.W. de Klerk shared the Nobel Peace Prize and in 1994 Mandela became South Africa's first black president.

Sophie and Hans Scholl (1921–1943 and 1918–1943). Students at the University in Munich, Germany, Sophie and Hans were instrumental in the mobilization of a student-led resistance to the Nazis known as the White Rose. Sophie and Hans were arrested and executed along with friend and colleague Christoph Probst.

Vandana Shiva (b. 1952). With a doctorate in physics, Shiva has founded research institutions and written many books on the environment and the harmful effects of globalization. She is the founder of Navdanya, an Indian NGO focused on the protection of heritage seeds, organic and traditional farming practices, fair trade economic agreements, biodiversity, and other areas of agricultural and environmental justice.

Aung San Suu Kyi (b. 1945). Chair of the Burmese National League for Democracy party, Suu Kyi was placed under house arrest for almost fifteen years. In 1991, she was awarded the Nobel Peace Prize for her struggle for peace and justice. She was liberated in 2010 and took a seat in parliament in 2012.

Thérèse of Lisieux (1873–1897). A Carmelite nun at the age of fifteen, Therese is one of the most popular saints in the Catholic Church. Her autobiography reveals her profound spirituality—the "Little Way" to the heart of God through a life of simplicity and growth in humbleness.

Archbishop Desmond Tutu (b. 1931). Born in South Africa, Archbishop Tutu was a major figure in the anti-apartheid movement in South Africa. He was appointed Archbishop of Cape Town, later retiring from the position to dedicate himself fully to leading the Truth and Reconciliation Commission, a groundbreaking method of bringing together a broken country.

Tony Walsh (1898–1994). A teacher in a Catholic residential school for first nations children, Walsh was cofounder of Benedict Labre House in Montreal, in 1952, which has the mission of hospitality for the poor and homeless. Walsh lived simply among the poor in radical accordance with the Gospels.

William Wilberforce (1759–1833). A member of the British Parliament in 1780, Wilberforce was seen as a preeminent figure in the drive to abolish slavery. His efforts contributed to the 1833 Slavery Abolition Act, eliminating slavery in most of the British Empire.

Malala Yousafzai (b. 1997). A native of Pakistan, twelve-year-old Malala spoke out when the Taliban would not allow girls to attend school. In 2012, she was shot on her school bus; she was sent to England for rehabilitation. She became an international leader for human rights, receiving the Nobel Peace Prize in 2014, when she was seventeen.

1. Nicholas Flood Davin, *Report on Industrial Schools for Indians and Half-Breeds*, quoted at Indigenous Foundations, http://indigenousfoundations.arts.ubc.ca/home/government-policy/the-residential-school-system.html.

2. University of British Columbia, "The Residential School System," indigenousfoundations.arts.ubc.ca; as well as "First Nations in Canada" from Aboriginal Affairs and Northern Development Canada, www.aadnc-aandc.gc.ca/en.

3. Etty Hillesum, *Etty Hillesum: An Interrupted Life (the Diaries, 1941–1943) and Letters from Westerbork* (New York: Henry Holt, 1996), p. 163.

4. Adapted from *Gaudium et Spes*, 16.

5. Hillesum, p. 256.

6. John F. Kennedy, Inaugural Speech, 1961, quoted in Thurston Clarke, *Ask Not: The Inauguration of John F. Kennedy and the Speech That Changed America* (New York: Penguin, 2010), n.p.

7. Aung San Suu Kyi, *Freedom from Fear: And Other Writings* (New York: Penguin, 2010), n.p.

8. The text continues, "so that you may be children of your Father in heaven" (Matthew 5:45, NJB). This is an amazing revelation. For who are the children of God? It is said earlier in this chapter, "Blessed are the peacemakers: they shall be recognized as children of God" (Matthew 5:9, NJB). This also corresponds with John chapter 1. Those who accept "the Word," the source of "light and

life" and "full of grace and truth" are given "power to become children of God. So whenever we read "children of God," we may understand this to be our vocation as peacemakers, as sources and seekers of light, life, truth, and grace in the world.

9. "Universal Declaration of Human Rights," Articles 1 and 2, http://www.un.org/en/documents/udhr/index.shtml.

10. Jonathan Tulloch, "Against the Tide," *The Tablet*, November 2014.

11. Hillesum, p. 178.

12. Hillesum, p. 156.

13. Maurice Zundel, *Un autre regard sur l'homme* (Paris: Jubile, 2005), p. 107.

14. Zundel, p. 121.

15. Zundel, p. 122.

16. Hillesum, p. 163.

17. Plato, *Apology*, 40c-d, quoted in Costica Bradatan, *Dying for Ideas: The Dangerous Lives of the Philosophers* (New York: Bloomsbury, 2015), p. 128.

18. Quoted in Jurgen Moltmann, *Jurgen Moltmann: Collected Readings* (Minneapolis: Augsburg Fortress, 2014), p. 201.

19. L'Arche Identity and Mission Statement.

20. Hillesum, p. 84.

21. M.K. Gandhi, *My Nonviolence*, 154, quoted in *Mahatma Gandhi, All Men Are Brothers* (New York: Bloomsbury, 2005), p. 49.

22. John Lennon and Paul McCartney, "Eleanor Rigby," *Revolver* (EMI, 1966).

23. Quoted in P.H. Coetzee, A.P.J. Roux, *The African Philosophy Reader* (London: Routledge, 2003), p. 416.

24. From Alcoholics Anonymous, *Twelve Steps and Twelve Traditions* (New York: Alcoholics Anonymous World Services, 2004).

25. Quoted in Breandan Leahy, Michael Mulvey, *Priests Today: Reflections on Identity, Life, and Ministry* (New York: New City, 2010), p. 102.

Did you know that SPCK
is a registered charity?

As well as publishing great books by leading Christian authors, we also . . .

. . . **make assemblies meaningful and fun for over a million children** by running www.assemblies.org.uk, a popular website that provides free assembly scripts for teachers. For many children, school assembly is the only contact they have with Christian faith and culture, and the only time in their week for spiritual reflection.

. . . **help prisoners to become confident readers** with our easy-to-read stories. Poor literacy is a huge barrier to rehabilitation. Prisoners identify with the believable heroes of our gritty fiction. At the same time, questions at the end of each chapter help them to examine their choices from a moral perspective and to build their reading confidence.

. . . **support student ministers overseas in their training.** We give them free, specially written theology books, the International Study Guides. These books really do make a difference, not just to students but to ministers and, through them, to a whole community.

Please support these great schemes: visit www.spck.org.uk/support-us to find out more.